WILDLIFE

Have you ever seen natterjack toads, Formosan deer or Vietnamese pot-bellied pigs? This book tells you where you can go to watch and learn about these animals, and is also full of other useful information on topics such as conservation, holidays and museums.

WILDLIFE

Elizabeth Holt and Molly Perham
Illustrated by Ross

Evans Brothers Limited London

First published 1979 by Evans Brothers Limited,
Montague House, Russell Square, London WC1B 5BX

British Library Cataloguing in Publication Data

Holt, Elizabeth
Wildlife nationwide. — (Activities nationwide).
1. Animals — Juvenile literature 2. Zoology — Great Britain — Juvenile literature
I. Title II. Perham, Molly III. Series
591.9'41 QL255

ISBN 0-237-44983-8

PRA 6559
Printed in Great Britain by
William Clowes & Sons Limited

Contents

About this Book

Being interested in natural history brings many benefits. You will have an absorbing and worthwhile interest which will continue throughout your life, you'll soon realize that the more you know the more there is to know, and the countryside and the creatures that live in it will benefit from your concern.

In recent years people have become more aware of the importance of our wildlife, and more concerned about its preservation. If you are keen to actually help in conservation, then there are plenty of clubs and societies mentioned in this book which would very much welcome your support. You'll not only be doing a great deal of good, but it will give you the opportunity to meet lots of other people with similar interests and to learn from their experience.

You probably have favourite haunts where you can watch wildlife, but we hope that we have suggested new places you can go to in your locality or which you can visit when you are on holiday. These are listed alphabetically in the text, and where possible the index gives you addresses, telephone numbers, and opening times. We have tried to provide as much information as possible, but we must stress that it really is important to check with the place in question or to get in touch with the local tourist office before setting off. Opening and closing times are always changing, some places close down with very little notice, and we wouldn't want you to have a wasted journey, especially as several of the sites we have mentioned are in very remote areas.

Note that you normally have to book for many of the sites run by the Royal Society for the Protection of Birds, but this cannot be done through headquarters. You must get in touch with local branches.

Aquaria and Dolphinaria

Twenty-four species of whales, porpoises and dolphins have been recorded off the British coasts. The best place for spotting whales is off the west coast of Scotland, especially the Hebrides. From Skye and Mull, from mainland resorts like Mallaig, Gairloch and Ullapool, or off the Cornish coast you may spot Killer or Pilot Whales, the Common Porpoise, or the White-beaked Dolphin. Of course, it's much easier to visit a dolphinarium to see these creatures, and you'll find it both instructive and entertaining.

Anyone gazing at a fishmonger's shop in this country would think that there are only about twenty species of fish and crustaceans to be found in the waters around our coast, but actually there are hundreds of different creatures. The best way to find out just what does live in the sea is to go to an aquarium. Some specialize in local fish, others include tropical fish.

We have suggested some dolphinaria and aquaria to visit, but practically every zoo and many bird gardens have fish, penguins, sea lions, and often dolphins as well.

Organizations

Green Peace, 47 Whitehall, London SW1 is an organization for those who are passionately concerned about whale hunting, the preservation of seals, and the need for conservation.

Places to visit

Anstruther: Scottish Fisheries Museum is an award-winning museum concerned with the fishing industry which also has a marine aquarium.
Bewdley: *see* Safari Parks
Blackpool: *see* Butterflies, Bees, Insects and Moths
Bolton: Bolton Aquarium has a comprehensive collection of fish.
Bournemouth: Russell-Cotes Museum and Art Gallery *see* Museums.
Bourton-on-the-Water: *see* Bird Gardens
Brighton: Brighton Aquarium and Dolphinarium has hundreds of marine, tropical and freshwater fish, sea lions, turtles and other exhibits, and a really splendid 1000-seater indoor dolphinarium.
Brixham: Brixham Aquarium has specimens of fish caught in local waters including sting and electric rays, sharks and octopus. It also has a trawling exhibition which explains the fishing methods used.
Cilfrew: *see* Bird Gardens
Exmouth: Exmouth Aquarium has a 60-year-old turtle amongst an interesting collection of local and tropical marine life.
Fladbury: *see* Bird Gardens
Godshill: Natural History Collection, private marine and tropical aquarium and a natural history collection is well worth visiting on the Isle of Wight.
Great Cumbrae Island: University Marine Biology Station isn't easy to get to, but if you manage it you'll find the trip was well worth while. There's a ferry from Largs.
Liverpool: Merseyside County Museum has a good aquarium.
London: Horniman Museum has a well-stocked aquarium.
Looe: Looe Aquarium has local marine specimens. You'll be impressed at the numbers and variety to be found within one mile of the shoreline.
Manchester: Manchester Museum has an aquarium with snakes, alligators and lizards as well as fish.
Millport: Robertson Museum and Aquarium has exhibits illustrating the marine life of the Clyde sea area.
Morecambe: Marineland Oceanarium and Aquarium has several dolphin shows every day during the holiday season. You can

also see sea lions, penguins, turtles, alligators, reptiles, and tropical and cold-water fish.
Newquay: Newquay Marine Aquarium has live locally caught fish and crustaceans.
Paignton: Paignton Seashore Aquarium has a unique collection of living seashore exhibits as well as static exhibits: fascinating if you are planning to explore beaches and rock pools.
Penzance: Penzance Aquarium illustrates the marine life of the area.
Plymouth: Plymouth Marine Biological Association Aquarium shouldn't be missed. It has one of the finest collections of marine animals in Europe, and is a major centre for research.
Port Erin: Marine Biological Station, used for teaching and research, has an aquarium with local fishes and invertebrates.
Portsmouth: Cumberland House Museum and Aquarium concentrates on the natural history and biology of the Hampshire basin.
Prescot: *see* Safari Parks
Redcar: Zetland Museum has an aquarium, the world's oldest lifeboat, and also shows the history of sea rescue and fishing. The museum organizes seashore field history trips.
St Ives: St Ives Aquarium is small but very interesting, and concentrates on locally caught exhibits.
Scarborough: Scarborough Zoo and Marineland has eager performing dolphins, as well as a zoo with a representative collection of animals.
Skegness: Natureland Marine Zoo has tropical and North Sea fish, sea lions, penguins, free-flight tropical birds, a wildfowl pool, and a children's corner.
Teignmouth: Teignmouth Aqualand has an interesting collection of marine life and exotic creatures, mainly from local waters.
Thrapston: Thrapston Bird Gardens and Fish Centre has native and tropical fish. The birds are well housed and organized, and you will see a large number of different species, all happily swooping around.
Torbay: Torbay Aqualand has a large collection of tropical and local marine life.
Whipsnade: *see* Zoos, Wildlife Parks, and Farms
Windsor: *see* Safari Parks
Woburn: *see* Safari Parks

Bird Gardens

If you are interested in seeing a wide variety of birds from all over the world – tropical birds, exotic birds, birds of prey, penguins, and so on, then there are a lot of bird gardens and aviaries throughout the country that you can visit, as well as collections in general zoos. Many of these birds fly, stalk, flutter or waddle freely around parks and gardens, whilst others are kept in special aviaries. You'll find plenty of information about unusual birds on identification cards and charts, so you shouldn't have any trouble in finding out their names and which country they come from.

Places to visit
Abbotsbury: Abbotsbury Gardens, covering about 17 acres, has pheasants, peacocks, budgerigars and other ornamental birds wandering around the flowering plants and shrubs in these very pleasant gardens.
Abbotsbury: Abbotsbury Swannery is the home of at least 500 swans, and it attracts many wild birds too. This swannery was established hundreds of years ago by Benedictine monks

on the River Fleet near Chesil Beach. No doubt the monks enjoyed watching these graceful birds, but they probably enjoyed eating them even more, as they were a much appreciated winter food in medieval times. Now the birds breed in peace, and if you go round about June you'll see newly-hatched cygnets.

Axbridge: Ambleside Water Gardens and Aviaries have two ornamental lakes in lovely gardens where wildfowl congregate. Small children will enjoy watching guinea pigs and rabbits scurrying across the lawns, noses twitching at the smell of sandwiches. You can also wander through a good walk-through aviary.

Birmingham: Edgbaston Botanical Gardens has a collection of tropical birds in outdoor aviaries, all in pleasant gardens planted with many interesting and unusual shrubs.

Blackpool: *see* Butterflies, Bees, Insects and Moths

Blagdon Hill: Widcombe Bird Gardens occupy a 20 acre site. Flamingoes, storks, peafowl, parakeets, waterfowl and many exotic birds live there, some in aviaries, others at liberty. If you have young children with you, they'll love the play area with miniature ponies, pigmy goats, and llamas.

Bourton-on-the-Water: Birdland Zoo Gardens has the largest and most varied collection of penguins anywhere, and you can get fascinating views of them through underwater viewing facilities. There's a tropical house with humming birds and other tropical birds enjoying the colourful flowers and plants. You'll see other birds at liberty, many of them having appeared on radio and television. Don't miss the unique shell-land while you are there.

Brean: Brean Down Garden is set at the foot of Brean Down, close to the long sandy beach. You'll see up to 300 birds from all over the world.

Bury St Edmunds: Norton Bird Gardens, about seven miles north-east of the town, has a good collection of tropical birds and wildfowl kept in lovely gardens. There's a tropical house too.

Cilfrew: Penscynor Wildlife Park has, quite rightly, won two tourist awards. There are over 1500 birds in this 15 acre park, a tropical house, and a pets' corner where the penguins flip-flop amongst the visitors. Have a look at the tropical fish while you are there.

Conlig: Lindos Bird Farm has aviaries with over 800 tropical birds like macaws, rosellas, budgerigars and finches.
Cookstown: *see* Butterflies, Bees, Insects and Moths
Coton: Coton Wildlife Gardens surround a 17th century house. There are a lot of wildfowl, cranes, flamingoes and other amusing and colourful birds around the lawns, lake and water gardens.
Coventry: Coombe Abbey Bird Garden has a collection of talking birds, trained birds of prey, free-flying cockatoos, and other birds. The pets' corner will attract younger children.
Cranham: Prinknash Bird Park, occupying about 9 acres of beautiful parkland, has around 700 birds. You can see flocks of geese, peacocks, swans including Indian blues, cranes, pheasants and others. Many feed from the hand, so watch your sandwiches. While you are there don't overlook the small animals like goats and Jacob sheep, and admire the stunning views over the Severn valley.
Darlington: South Park has a lake with wildfowl and an aviary. There's a mile-long nature trail to follow. There's a free guide which you can pick up in the park or the Central library.
Farnham: Birdworld Zoological Gardens has many varieties of birds including parrots, flamingoes, kestrels, toucans and tropical finches in a 5 acre garden, many of them housed in large flights and paddocks. Feeding time is usually 11.15.
Fladbury: Delamere Bird Gardens has a good collection of tropical birds as well as fish, reptiles, and pet animals. There's also a superb display of mounted butterflies and moths.
Forest Row: Spring Hill Wildfowl Park consists of a 10 acre garden around a 15th century farmhouse. It holds up to 1000 birds, including some rare ducks and geese.
Guilsborough: Guilsborough Grange Bird and Pet Park has exotic birds and wildfowl, a children's playground, and a pets' corner with pony and donkey rides for younger visitors. It's all set in pleasantly wooded countryside.
Halland: Bentley Wildfowl Collection really is worth a visit. There are over 100 species of wildfowl, many of them rare, and lots of ornamental and exotic birds. The grounds are lovely and peaceful.
Harewood: Harewood House and Bird Garden is set in a park landscaped by Capability Brown. The 4 acre bird garden holds about 200 species. Go and look at the splendid World of

Butterflies while children can have fun in the playground.
Hayle: Bird Paradise has rare and endangered species of birds – the Mexican thick-billed parrot, and the Hyacinthine macaw, for example. Admire the brilliant free-flying parrots, have a ride on a donkey, and look in at the children's zoo. When you've had enough of that, there's still a craft village and a miniature railway to see.
Henley-in-Arden: Henley Bird Gardens are situated in the beautiful grounds of an Elizabethan country house. It is the home of about 300 brightly coloured and often noisy tropical birds.
Ipsden: Wellplace Bird Farm has over 100 species of birds, and there are a number of small animals like badgers, otters, foxes and monkeys to interest and amuse you.
Kelling: Kelling Park Aviaries has a good collection of European and tropical birds including ornamental pheasants, cranes, and cockatoos. Its speciality are the lorikeets.
Lilford: Lilford Park has aviaries which were originally constructed in 1861. They are full of hundreds of birds, and there are also large numbers of wildfowl. You can see the animals in the children's farm, while the really young can get rid of surplus energy in an adventure playground.
London: Syon Park, the famous garden centre, has a walk-through aviary and an aquarium.
Marden: Verne Estate Garden and Aviaries has macaws, parrots, cranes, hornbills and many other exotic and wild birds as well as animals like llamas, sheep, goats and Highland cattle.
Melton Mowbray: Stapleford Park has a beautiful lake with an island bird sanctuary. There is also a small zoo and lion reserve.
Muncaster: Muncaster Castle has bird gardens with lots of tropical and ornamental birds, and a flamingo pool where the birds stand stiffly at attention on one leg. There's also a Himalayan bear pit to visit, and a good nature trail to follow.
Northampton: Abingdon Park has ornamental and game birds in the landscaped park and ornamental gardens. The house itself is now a museum.
Padstow: Tropical Bird and Butterfly Gardens has superb gardens with tropical and sub-tropical plants. You can stroll through a tropical house with free-flying birds zooming around.

During the summer months you'll see lots of butterflies.
Rode: Tropical Bird Gardens has up to 180 species of tropical birds in aviaries. The 17 acres of grounds has lakes, lawns, shrubs and trees, with small animals and some birds. Younger children can enjoy the pets' corner and ride on a donkey.
St Florence: Manor House Wildlife and Leisure Park has won a special tourist award. Look at the birds and the fish, and at the small animal collection which includes monkeys, otters, and deer. The gardens are a pleasure to drift around, and you might be lucky enough to see one of the occasional demonstrations of crafts.
St Lawrence: Tropical Bird Park has many species of tropical birds, and you can admire their brilliance in walk-through aviaries. Flamingoes and cranes tend to gather around the large pond.
Seaview: Flamingo Park Bird Sanctuary is a refuge for hundreds of waterfowl, and you'll also see pheasants, geese and swans, many of them very tame. There's a special British and foreign bird house, and a pets' corner.
Stagsden: Stagsden Bird Gardens covers about 8 acres of pleasant countryside. It concentrates on the breeding of rare birds, particularly pheasants and old breeds of poultry, but there are also large numbers of waterfowl and other birds. There's excellent information on names and countries of origin, and a very helpful staff ready to answer questions. Whatever you do, don't miss the nursery coops in the East garden.
Strangford: Castle Ward has a wildfowl collection in really fine gardens. You'll find the information centre very helpful.
Thrapston: *see* Aquaria
Waddesdon: Waddesdon Manor has extensive grounds and a garden with a fine aviary with free-flying birds. There's a small herd of deer as well.
Weston Underwood: Flamingo Gardens and Zoological Park has an impressive collection of all sorts of birds. There could be 1000 at a time, representing about 200 different species. The park has some mammals too, including dwarf zebras and llamas.
Wimborne Minster: Merley Tropical Bird Gardens has lovely lawns and gardens covering over 3 acres with more than 100 species of birds on display. There's a pets' corner for young visitors to admire.

Birds in the Wild

The secret of successful bird-watching is to know where to look for which species. Very roughly, their habitats can be divided into three – land, waterside, and water. In agricultural country you'll see a number of different kinds of birds, and if the area includes marshes, lakes, rivers or wetlands, you could spot up to fifty species in a few hours. Waterside habitats include swamps, bogs, the margins of lakes, rivers, saltmarshes, and flats. Birds that feed over open water must, of course, find somewhere to breed on land.

Many birds are protected in this country, and a lot of bird sanctuaries have been established so that they can live and breed undisturbed by man. Some of these sanctuaries have restricted entry, and often it's best to be a member of a club or society. Others cannot be visited at all. This might seem hard, but it's the only way that we can ensure that rare and endangered species will survive and breed here.

Really, to get the most out of bird-watching, you should join one of the societies mentioned below. You'll get far more out of your interest if you share it with others, you'll have the added bonus of learning from other people's experience, and you'll also have the opportunity on going on expeditions and holidays, and joining in social activities.

As you can imagine, to list all the places where you can watch birds is an impossible task – after all, you can do it from your own back garden, and who wants a list of everyone's back garden? What we've tried to do is to suggest areas all over the country. Many of them are difficult to reach, unfortunately, but they are all places where you'll see birds that are most unlikely to appear in your garden.

Organizations

British Ornothologists' Club, c/o Zoological Society of London, Regent's Park, London NW1.

British Trust for Ornithology, Beech Grove, Tring, Hertfordshire, is the body concerned with scientific bird study for amateurs. Members receive a quarterly journal, *Bird Study*, and a newsletter.

Wildfowl Trust, Slimbridge, Gloucestershire, Tel Cambridge 333, was founded by Peter Scott in 1946 for research and education, and for the conservation of wild birds. As well as the headquarters at Slimbridge there are six other centres open to the public at Arundel, Burscough, Caerlaverock, Peterborough, Welney and Washington. Members of the Trust have free admission to these bird sanctuaries, and two copies a year of *Wildfowl News*. You can also adopt a duck – one of the thousands examined and ringed each year. If there is news of your duck after it has been released, you'll be informed. Mind you, if you don't fancy a duck, you could support a swan or a barnacle goose.

Young Ornithologists' Club, RSPB, the Lodge, Sandy, Bedfordshire, is the junior branch of the Royal Society for the Protection of Birds. The subscription is low, and very low indeed for group membership, and you'll be able to go birdwatching with others, often to reserves not open to the general public. You'll also be given a kestrel arm badge, a colourful magazine, *Bird Life*, which comes out four times a year, and a newsletter. On joining you'll get a list of adult members in your part of the country who will be happy to take junior members on expeditions. The club offers holiday courses, and there are remarkably varied projects, ranging from bird censuses to the examination of pellets, competitions, books to buy and a free leaflet on feeding garden birds. The 104 acres of the headquarters at Sandy, Bedfordshire are open daily to members. There is heathland, woodland, ponds, and parks to wander round, nature trails, an observation hide, a nature discovery room, and a shop.

Other Organizations
Most nature reserves are owned or managed by the organizations below:
National Trust, 42 Queen Anne's Gate, London SW1
Nature Conservancy, 19 Belgrave Square, London SW1
Royal Society for the Protection of Birds, The Lodge, Sandy, Bedfordshire
Society for the Promotion of Nature Reserves (for the County Naturalists' Trusts), The Green, Nettleham, Lincoln

Places to visit
Ainsdale: Ainsdale National Nature Reserve, not far from Southport, consists of pine woods and sand dunes. It's the home of many species of birds, butterflies, red squirrels, and of the rare natterjack toad. Keen observers may well see pygmy shrews and foxes too.
Antrim: Shane's Castle Railway and Nature Reserve has a wide variety of wildlife with hides so that you can get a really good look at species. Kingfishers and sparrowhawks can be seen. You can also chug around the reserve on a narrow gauge railway.
Arran: *see* Deer
Arundel: Arundel Branch of the Wildfowl Trust covers 60 acres with ponds and lakes where you might see over 700 ducks, swans and geese from all over the world. There's a special area of 20 acres which is a sanctuary for birds, and the carefully placed hides give you the opportunity to watch them at close quarters. Among the many species are sandpipers, redshanks, and the greenshanks.
Ayre: The Ayres on the Isle of Man has a really good Visitors Centre with displays giving information on wildlife habitats, maps and aerial photographs, and illustrations of species to watch out for. You can follow a trail and see Arctic and common tern, the rarer little tern, gannets, and sometimes, grey seals.
Ballymacormick Point: Cockle Island, off the point, is a haven for a number of species of seabirds. Note that access is restricted during the nesting season which lasts from May to July.
Bass Rock: Bass Rock, 350 feet high off North Berwick, is

inhabited by thousands of noisy seabirds. There are nearly six thousand pairs of breeding gannets there, and in the summer there are fulmar, puffin, razorbill, shag, kittiwake and others. Boat trips from North Berwick will give you the chance to observe, but if you hope to visit, you should get in touch with the Scottish Ornithologists' Club which runs excursions most summers.

Birkenhead: Arrowe Park, with its large lake, has established a bird sanctuary.

Birmingham: Cannon Hill Nature Centre has grounds resembling natural habitat to attract wild birds and butterflies. There are also displays of living animals of the British Isles.

Blacktoft Sands: This new RSPB reserve in South Humberside has wading birds, duck, bearded tits, and short-eared owls — the only owls to hunt by day.

Blakeney: Blakeney Point Nature Reserve is a wildfowl breeding area. You'll spot many species of seabirds including Artic tern, ringed plover, oyster catchers and others. You might even see seals basking on the sandbanks. Access is from Blakeney Quay according to the tide.

Brancaster Staithe: This National Nature Reserve has breeding colonies of terns, but throughout the year it is thronged with birds of all kinds — merlins, short-eared owls, oyster-catchers, wigeon, grey plovers, godwits — an endless list. Access is by boat (there's a timetable on the quay) and is unrestricted, except over the terneries in the breeding season.

Brill: Bourstall Duck Decoy and Nature Reserve attracts many species of birds. Demonstrations at the decoy are held on Sundays at 16.00 and on Bank Holidays at 11.00, 12.00, 14.00 and 16.00. There's an excellent nature trail based on the need for conservation of wildlife in Europe.

Brodick: Goatfell is the highest peak on Arran. If you can manage to get there look for golden eagles, hawks and harriers.

Bridlington: Go four miles east of the town for the Danes Dyke Nature Trail which runs along woodland and the coast. Many birds nest here, so take binoculars and be quiet. There's a free guide available from the information centre in Garrison Street.

Brook: Here on the Isle of Wight there's a Local Look exhibition in August with leaflets on three nature trails — you'll find that there's a wide variety of birdlife to observe. Go to the Isle of Wight Tourist Board for further information.

Buckden: Grafham Water, about three miles south west of Huntingdon, is a huge man-made lake where you can see a wide variety of birds. Watch for black tern in spring, Bewick's swan in winter, and redshanks and greenshanks in spring and autumn. There are good vantage points close to the car parks.
Burscough: Martin Mere Branch of the Wildfowl Trust is the place to see thousands of tame birds and wildfowl in this 360 acre marshland area which includes pens, paddocks, and a wild area. The man-made mere is easily visible from carefully situated hides. There's an astonishing large log cabin with a grass roof where geese graze, quite undisturbed by visitors. There is also an excellent Visitors Centre and an exhibition hall.
Burton Bradstock: Burton Mere is a marvellous area to observe numerous migrating birds. This can be reached by walking along the beach from Burton Bradstock.
Caerlaverock: Caerlaverock Branch of the Wildfowl Trust, a reserve not far from the Castle, is an area of saltmarsh and sandy foreshore between Lochar Water and the River Neath. It is alive with wildfowl, particularly in the winter, and has excellent facilities for bird-watching with well-situated hides, observation towers, and an observatory. Watch for huge flocks of pink-footed geese, barnacle geese, wigeon and pintail among the many species that arrive here. Access is unrestricted except in the sanctuary.
Calf of Man: This is a small island on the Isle of Man belonging to the National Trust. It's both a bird observatory and a nature reserve. You can only reach it via Port St Mary or Port Erin. Before visiting the observatory get in touch with the Secretary of the Manx Museum at Douglas. You'll see large colonies of sea birds and many birds of passage.
Canterbury: Bleans Wood, about three miles from the city, is a bird sanctuary which also has a nature trail.
Castle Douglas: Threave House and Wildfowl Reserve is a roosting and feeding place for many species of wild geese and ducks. Access is restricted from November to March at selected points to avoid disturbing the birds.
Claw Moor: Claw Moor Wildfowl Observation Hide is in an area of forest between Holsworth, Hatherleigh, and Okehampton. All wildlife – particularly many species of wildfowl – are attracted by this 5 acre man-made pond. However, only really keen naturalists or recognized societies can get permits to visit

this very interesting hide.
Cley-next-the-Sea: Cley Marshes Nature Reserve, covering 435 acres, is justly famous. Over 275 species have been recorded within the parish. The main bird-watching area is between the villages of Cley and Salthouse, but wherever you go you'll see birds. The sanctuary is provided with several hides offering superb views over the whole reserve.
Coldstream: Hirsel House houses the sanctuary of Dundock Wood.
Colchester: Kingsford Bridge Marsh Reserve, south of the city, is the home for numerous species of birds. Needle's Eye Wood has nesting birds such as the hawfinch, nuthatch and nightingale.
Colchester: Fingrinhoe Nature Reserve, run by Essex Naturalists' Trust, is about five miles south west of the city on the west bank of the Colne estuary. There's a wide variety of birdlife, a good interpretive centre, and you can follow two nature trails.
Cookstown: *see* Butterflies, Bees, Insects and Moths
Copeland Islands: These form a bird sanctuary with many species both nesting and resting here. It's not easy to reach from Donaghadee, but worth the effort. Watch out for basking seals.
Croydon: Coombe Wood has a bird sanctuary. The woodside ramble is strenuous – there's thirteen miles of it, although there is a shorter version for those who aren't quite so fit. You can get a guide from either the café at the wood or from local libraries.
Dunwich: Minsmere Bird Sanctuary is within the Dunwich Heath area. The sandy cliffs, heathland, beach and a small lake all attract many species of birds.
Fair Isle: Fair Isle Bird Observatory on this isolated island between Shetland and Orkney has about 300 species of migrating birds. Among those that breed here are Arctic skuas, razorbills, and fulmars. It's not an easy place to get to, but there are two sailings a week in the summer from Shetland.
Farne Islands: *see* Seals and Otters
Fetlar: This is the smallest of the main Shetland Islands, and is now a large nature reserve. The RSPB reserve may only be visited from May-August. Apart from the famous snowy owl, there are other rare birds to be seen – in fact, it swarms with birdlife. Note that you must contact the warden at Bealance

Bothy on arrival. There are regular boat and air services from Lerwick.

Flamborough Head: The Head appears spectacular, projecting as it does from a smooth coastline. It offers nesting sites to large numbers of kittiwakes. There's always a rich variety of birds, but look especially for divers, fulmars and auks in the spring.

Glanton: Glanton World Bird Research Station, nine miles west of Alnwick, is certainly worth visiting. You'll see serious bird study, hear bird recordings, and be able to see a fascinating reference collection of living birds relating to their association with man from prehistory to today. Birds are treated in the first-aid and release centre. In fact, birds are everywhere. If you want them to eat out of your hand, the station even provides free food.

Glendaruel Forest: There are wildlife observation hides here. Get in touch with the Forestry Office at Tighnabruaich, Strathclyde for watching or photography.

Gwenffrwd: Gwenffrwd and Dinas Forest is managed by the RSPB. You can see redstarts, pied flycatchers, buzzards, merlin and many other species. There is a nature trail at the Dinas. Check if you want to go in the RSPB reserve. Access is usually by permit four days a week in the summer.

Gwydyr Forest: Clogwyn Cyrau Observation Hide gives you the chance to observe wildlife at close quarters. There's a birdwatching trail too. Tickets and information are available from the Gwydyr Visitors Centre.

Handa Island: Handa Island Bird Sanctuary, off the Isle of Scourie, can only be reached with the help of local boatmen, but for keen birdwatchers it will be worth the effort. It is alive with vast numbers of fulmars, kittiwakes, auks, shags and gulls. As in other places, there's a bonus in being a member of the RSPB since there is accommodation in a well-equipped hut.

Hickling: Hickling Broad Water Trail and Nature Reserve, run by Norfolk Naturalists' Trust, covers over 1300 acres with about 370 acres of open water. Breeding birds include shovellers, sedge warblers, heron, bittern and snipe. You can go on a two hour trip in a traditional reed lighter to various points including a unique tree hide, or follow the water trail which starts from the Pleasure Boat Inn. Get in touch with the Trust for more details. Permits are issued in advance for the reserve.

Holme-next-the-Sea: Holme Nature Reserve, consisting of over 400 acres, has hides overlooking wader pools. These may be used from Wednesday-Monday in April-October. You can also go on self-guided walks from May-September. Admission is by permit issued in advance.
Holywell: Gull Rocks are off Penhale Point, about three miles from Newquay in Cornwall. Take binoculars if you hope to observe the mixed colony of auks.
Inverpolly: Bog, moorland, cliffs and woodland provide shelter for a wide variety of birdlife. The Information Centre is concerned with the general ecology of the area.
Kielder: Kielder Castle, near Forest Drive in Northumberland, has a wildlife observation hide. The Chief Forester has details of charges and bookings. There's a good Visitors Centre too.
Kinross: Vane Farm Nature Reserve on the south shore of Loch Leven has literally thousands of wild geese and ducks between September and April. There is an excellent Nature Centre with displays, and there are observation facilities and a nature trail.
Liverpool: Hilbre Island is a bird sanctuary open throughout the year, but access is limited by the tide. You can go on a long but rewarding nature trail lasting about three hours. Watch out for wading birds and Atlantic seals.
Llandudno: Great Orme's Head has a good cliff breeding colony. In the summer it's the haunt of guillemot, razorbill, puffin and fulmar, and in the autumn the Manx shearwater, scoter and gannet.
Loch Druidilbeg: This is a nature reserve in South Uist, and is an important breeding ground for greylag geese. You'll need a permit to come here in the breeding season.
Loch Garten: Here is one of the few places where you can watch ospreys through fixed binoculars in an observation hut. Access to the sanctuary is permitted only along the track leading to the hut. You can admire these birds from mid-April to mid-October.
Loch of the Lowes: Here's another place where you can hope to see ospreys fishing. The Visitors Centre will help you to understand the ecology of the region.
Lough Neagh: Oxford Island Nature Reserve is a place to see kestrels, great crested grebes, and wild swans. There's a good nature trail with a free guide. Guided tours can be arranged.

Markethill: Gosford Forest Park has a good nature trail. There are ornamental ponds, a river and a wildfowl enclosure. You have to pay to go on the trail, but the guide is provided free.
Needles: This famous headland on the Isle of Wight consists of nearly 40 acres of downland overlooking the Needles. You'll see numerous sea birds. You can only reach it on foot from either the Downs or the Alum Bay car park.
Newtown: Newtown Marsh on the Isle of Wight is an area of 130 acres which was flooded in 1954. There are public footpaths with excellent views of the marshes. Keen spotters should see waders in the spring, gulls in the summer, golden and grey plovers, greenshanks and ruff in the autumn, and a wide variety of species in the winter.
Newtownstewart: *see* Deer
Northey Island: Northey Island, covering 260 acres in the Blackwater estuary near Maldon in Essex, consists largely of saltings which are home to many species of water and shore birds in the winter, and to the shelduck, the common tern, waders, and others in the summer.
Noss: Noss Nature Reserve is on an impressive island encircled by high cliffs. It's a breeding ground for auks, gulls, gannets, and many other birds. There are frequent trips around the island from Lerwick. The reserve run by the RSPB can be visited most days of the week from June-August. You'll see details of the ferries in Lerwick Harbour.
Orford: Havergate Island in Suffolk is a mecca for those who want to see avocet, but there are many other species to spot. Waders are attracted by the marshy conditions. Access to the island is by boat accompanied by the warden. Permits must be booked in advance from the RSPB, and very few visitors a day are allowed in the reserve.
Peakirk: Peakirk Branch of the Wildfowl Trust has waterfowl gardens on the site of an old osier bed. They have about 600 wildfowl representing about 80 species, many of which are rare. At Borough Fen you'll see a duck decoy where hundreds of birds are caught, ringed and released. At the Gate House you'll find a really good wildlife exhibition.
Poole: Brownsea Island, owned by the National Trust, can only be reached from Poole Quay or Sandbanks, and although you can wander around the island, access to the reserve is restricted to guided parties. There is a public hide near the

quay equipped with a telescope, and the nature trail is always open.

Ranworth: Broadland Conservation Centre in Norfolk has a floating gallery moored on Ranworth Inner Broad. You can bird-watch, and see displays on conservation and history of the Broad. The Centre is approached by a nature trail that takes you through woodlands.

Rathlin Island: The cliffs that stretch for miles are the home of vast numbers of raucous sea birds. Up to 20,000 guillemots live here, and you'll see razorbill, puffin, buzzard and many other species. In the winter flocks of greylag and barnacle geese arrive. One of the best viewing spots is from the west lighthouse. You can reach the island by boat from Ballycastle.

Rhandirmwyn: Dinas Nature Trail is about three miles from here in an oakwood gorge on the River Towy. You'll see masses of birds including red kite. There's an Information Centre at the car park, and information is posted along the trail. Strong shoes and a lot of hush are recommended.

Sandy: *see* RSPB in the introduction to this section. Those not members of the RSPB are welcome.

Skegness: Gibraltar Point Nature Reserve, about three miles from Skegness, is used for the study of bird migration. Throughout the year there are numerous species of birds to spot. Passerines include flycatchers, warblers and chats, and in winter there are always waders, snow buntings, and sea duck. There are observation hides, a nature trail open from April to October, and a Station Visitors Centre. Keep an eye open for seals on the off-shore sandbanks.

Skomer Island: Two nature walks start at North Haven. The boat embarkation point is at Martin's Haven. Obviously you've got to pay for the boat trip and the landing fee. You can either buy a guide and follow the trails which will take you through the nature reserve where you can see bird colonies, or you can go on guided walks on Wednesdays from May-August.

South Walsham: Fairhaven Garden Trust has lovely gardens, water gardens, and a fish-pond. You can visit the bird sanctuary at certain times by arrangement with the Warden.

Selborne: This Hampshire village, the home of Gilbert White, has the famous zig-zag path to the Hanger covered in beech trees. Look for goldcrests and warblers in the summer.

Stewartby: Stewartby Lake, five miles from Bedford and close to the village, used to be a clay pit. In the spring you'll see a surprising number of species including shoveller and black tern in the spring, and a gull roost in the winter.

Strangford Lough: This reserve is protected by the National Trust. There are hides so that you can watch swans, geese, ducks and waders. Up to 130 species can be observed, and about half the world's population of Brent geese choose it as a winter refuge.

Slimbridge: Slimbridge Branch of the Wildfowl Trust, established in 1946 by Peter Scott, is famous for the many thousands of ducks, geese and swans that visit it. It also houses a vast collection of wildfowl, and has made a unique contribution to conservation. There are two decoys, superb viewing facilities, a tropical house with humming birds and other exotic species, and interesting permanent exhibitions.

Stodmarsh: Stodmarsh National Nature Reserve in Kent, covering just over 400 acres of alluvial marshland, is on the south bank of the River Stour. There is access from Stodmarsh village near the Red Lion, but the right of way is usually impassable. However, you can use the flood barrier and the Lampen Wall for observation. In the summer look out for bittern, shelduck, warblers, and others.

Tentsmuir Point: This nature reserve between the River Tay and the River Earn is alive with birds. You'll see large flocks of long-tailed duck in early spring, eider and scoter in summer, and many species throughout the autumn and winter.

Tring: Tring Reservoirs include Startops End, Marsworth, Tringford and Wilstonal and form part of the Grand Union Canal. The 50 acre reserve includes banks and woodlands. Access is restricted, but there are numerous public footpaths, all clearly marked. There's an excellent nature trail starting at Startops End, Tring. A guide is available at weekends.

Washington: Washington Waterfowl Park is owned by the Wildfowl Trust. The refuge has over 100 different kinds of birds with a special emphasis on those from North America. The woods contain wild bird feeding stations, and comfortable hides provide excellent views over the reed beds and ponds of the wild area. Ducks and waders take sanctuary here particularly in the winter or when on migration.

Welney: Welney Branch of the Wildfowl Trust is a must for bird lovers. On the 800 acres of the Ouse Washes over 1000

Bewick's swans spend the winter, and thousands of other birds shelter. There are hides, a spacious observatory, and you can even arrange to watch swans by floodlight in the evening.
Wicken Fen: Three miles west of Southam there are 730 acres of wetland reserve with sedge, thorn and weed, a tangle that is almost impenetrable, although there are wide paths to walk along. It has a wide variety of bird, insect and plant life. The reserve has an observation tower. Entrance is free, but you have to leave a deposit and pay a small charge if you want to use the tower. Find the warden at the cottage down the Wicken Fen track to make arrangements. You can also buy a guide from him if you want to go on the nature trail which will offer you the opportunity to see birds you might have missed.
Woolhope Hall: Haugh Wood, not far from Hereford, is owned by the Forestry Commission and the National Trust. You can see warblers, nightjar, nightingale and woodcock. There is a good nature trail starting on the north side of Fownhope Road.
Worksop: Clumber Park, just over two miles from the town, has three large lakes which attract a great number of winter wildfowl. In the summer look out for redstart, goldcrest, warblers, and nightingales.

Books

Books useful for identification are:
AA/Readers' Digest Book of British Birds
The Birds of Britain and Europe, Heinzel, Fitter & Parslow (Collins)
Birds of Sea and Coast, Lars Jonsson (Penguin Nature Guides)
Birds of Wood, Park and Garden, Lars Jonsson (Penguin Nature Guides)
A Field Guide to the Birds of Britain and Europe, Peterson, Mountford & Hollom (Collins)
The Hamlyn Guide to Birds of Britain and Europe, B Braun (Hamlyn)
RSPB Guide to British Birds, David Saunders (Hamlyn)
Books about migration are:
Bird Behaviour, J Sparks (Hamlyn All Colour Paperbacks)
Bird Count, Humphrey M Dobinson (Peacock Books)
Instructions for Young Ornithologists: Bird Migration, R Spencer (Museum Press)
Migration, O B Gregory (A Wheaton & Co)

Books about how to watch birds are:
Bird-Watching, Neil Ardley & Brian Hawkes (Macdonald Guidelines)
Collins Guide to Bird Watching, Richard Fitter (Collins)
Discovering Bird Watching, Jim Flegg (Shire Publications)

Butterflies, Bees, Insects and Moths

There are a number of places where you can see butterflies and moths fluttering around, and places where they are especially bred. Quite a number of museums have excellent displays of tropical and native butterflies, and although it seems a pity that these beautiful insects were caught and mounted, it does give you an opportunity to see species that will almost certainly never come your way.

If you want to encourage butterflies in your garden, you'll find that certain plants attract them, but do remember that although they might arrive in large numbers, they still need a chance to breed. If you can, persuade your parents to leave a small patch of thistles and weeds or get them to leave the grass and herbage at the bottom of hedges so that some species will find a natural habitat.

Places to visit
Beckley: The Saruman Museum has a unique butterfly exhibition.

Birmingham: Birmingham City Museum and Art Gallery has the important Kenrick lepidoptera collection.
Blackpool: Tower Buildings and Circus has beautiful butterfly gardens, an aquarium, a free-flight aviary, a small domestic zoo, and a parrot and monkey jungle.
Bournemouth: Rothesay Museum has a fine collection of butterflies and moths.
Cookstown: Drum Manor has a lovely butterfly garden, a heronr[illegible] red squirrels, a lake with wildfowl, and a helpful Information Centre.
Eastbourne: Beachy Head Nature Trail will lead you over lovely downland with superb views. There's a wide variety of plants and butterflies to observe, probably at their best in spring and summer. You can get a cheap guide at the start of the trail which is signposted from the B2103, or from the town's Information Centre.
Eastbourne: Towner Art Gallery has the very good Bell collectio[illegible] of British butterflies.
Fladbury: *see* Bird Gardens
Harewood: *see* Bird Gardens
Laxfield: Laxfield District Museum has an observation beehive.
London: Horniman Museum has an observation beehive, and a good collection of butterflies and moths.
Louth: Louth Naturalists, Antiquarians and Literary Society Museum has a fine display of butterflies and moths.
Mablethorpe: *see* British and European Collections and Farms.
Matlock: *see* British and European Collections and Farms.
Nottingham: Nottingham Natural History Museum has a really good new insect gallery as well as zoology exhibits. There are red and fallow deer in the park, and a signposted nature trail around the lake.
Olney: Emberton Park Nature Trail is a mile-long walk by a lake and riverside where you can expect to see butterflies, moths and birds, and if you are lucky, you'll find traces of the passage of otters and badgers. You can get a guide or a free leaflet from the park office. Try this walk in spring and summer to see butterflies.
Over Compton: Worldwide Butterflies Ltd operates from an Elizabethan country house. You can enter the breeding room

and watch butterflies emerge from chrysalises, saunter in the tropical jungle where they breed naturally and fly in exotic greenery, or walk in the palm house and pretend that you are abroad. You'll also find a butterfly house in the grounds.
Over Compton: Lullingstone Silk Farm, opened in 1932, has provided silk for royal robes at the last two coronations, and for four royal wedding dresses. You can watch silk farm rearing, learn about the history of silk, see reeling machinery in the filature, and find out just what happens to raw silk. For further information write to Worldwide Butterflies above, but head your letter Lullingstone Silk Farm.
Padstow: *see* Bird Gardens
Penrhyn: Penrhyn Castle has a collection of butterflies, insects, stuffed animals and birds.
Salcombe: Overbecks Museum has a good collection of butterflies.
Stoneleigh: British Beekeepers' Association runs the National Bee Garden at the National Agricultural Centre. On certain days you can stroll around the garden and gaze at the observation beehives. Do check that the garden is open before you set off.
Wickham Market: *see* British and European Collections and Farms.
Wookey Hole: Only two miles from Wells is the Ebbor Gorge Nature Reserve with a short nature trail through woodland and grassland which is the home of many species of butterflies. You can get a cheap guide from the Priddys Reserve car park.
Ystwyth Forest: Coed Alt Butterfly Reserve has a remarkable number of species of butterflies. The reserve is run jointly by the Forestry Commission and the West Wales Naturalists' Trust.

Books

British Butterflies – A Field Guide, Robert Goodden (David & Charles)
Butterflies, Robert Goodden (Hamlyn All Colour Paperbacks)
A Colour Guide to Familiar Butterflies, Caterpillars and Chrysalides, Josef Moucha (Octopus)
A Field Guide to the Butterflies of Britain and Europe, L G Higgins & N D Riley (Collins)
Field and Meadow Life, Leif Lyreborg (Blandford)
Insects in Colour, N D Riley (Blandford)
Looking at Butterflies, L Hugh Newman (Collins)

Deer

The deer that you are most likely to see roaming wild are the fallow deer, which are about three feet high and have white-spotted coats during the summer months, and the rose deer, which stand only about 26 inches high. The magnificent red deer, which stand about six feet high, are found in the highlands of Scotland and on stretches of moorland in Devon and Somerset. The stag's antlers may grow to three feet, and when it has twelve points to them, it is given the title of 'royal stag'. The winter coat of the red deer is brownish-grey to blend with its surroundings. Practically every zoo, wildlife centre and safari park have deer for you to admire, and there are many free-roaming herds in various parks, forests and nature reserves. Some of these are listed below.

Places to visit
Arran: You'll find impressive herds of wild red deer at the north end of this beautiful island. Some 2000 animals now inhabit 100 square miles. While you are there watch for the royals – those deer with twelve-pointed antlers. You'll find the Arran Nature Centre helpful over identification.
Belton: Belton House and Park has 600 acres of parkland with fallow deer. You can also observe Canada geese, send the younger children into the Jungle Wilderness Adventure Wood, and follow exciting lakeland and nature trails.

Berkeley: Berkeley Castle is the 12th century castle in which Edward II was brutally murdered. You can see the extensive deer park, visit the dungeons, be amazed at the medieval kitchens and other apartments, and wander round the gardens and see the Elizabethan bowling alley.
Chippenham: Dyrham Park, built between 1692 and 1702, has 263 acres of parkland with a herd of fallow deer roaming about.
Clatteringshaws Loch: Galloway Deer Museum is about five miles south of New Galloway. Galloway Forest Park on the A712 is one place to see these impressive animals. The museum explains the history of the red deer in Galloway very clearly, and you can drift around looking at other natural history exhibits.
Disley: Lyme Park, a lovely Elizabethan house with 18th and 19th century additions, has a large deer park. There's a good nature trail too. This starts near the car park.
Grange-over-Sands: Holker Hall has a park with red, fallow and rare Formosan deer. There's a children's farm and an adventure playground too.
Kinloch Glen: Isle of Rhum National Conservation Centre is concerned with the study of deer, and there are plenty to study – about 1500 at the last count. There's other wildlife for you to observe, including many birds. Mind you, it's not easy to get there. The boat service goes from Mallaig four times a week.
Knebworth: Knebworth House and Country Park has deer herds, bird gardens, a good adventure playground, and a miniature railway.
Knutsford: Tatton Park has large herds of fallow and red deer roaming freely, and you can see wildfowl on the mere. You can spend the day observing wildlife, fishing, swimming, sailing and wandering around a museum of veteran cars.
Loch Morlich: Glenmore Forest Park, about seven miles east of Aviemore on the A951, has Loch Morlich as its centre. Over 12,000 acres of pine and spruce shelter red deer, reindeer, wildcat, golden eagles and capercailzie.
London: Bushy Park is only separated from Hampton Court Park by a road, and so, if you are visiting the palace, why not stretch your legs and walk over to see deer and cattle grazing.
London: Richmond Park, created by Charles I in 1637, covers

2500 acres and is the home of 250 red and 350 fallow deer.
Ludlow: It's only two miles from Ludlow to Whitcliffe Wood where you can wander along a nature trail keeping a sharp look out for deer or even badgers. You can get a guide from the Forestry Commission, Whitcliffe Wood, Whitcliffe.
Lynford: Lynford Forest shelters red and roe deer. Follow the two mile nature trail and see if you can spot them. The trail is free, but there's a small charge for the guide which can be picked up from the car park east of the A134.
New Forest: This forest is vast and is a marvellous place to observe wildlife. You'll see Sika, red, roe and fallow deer, the famous New Forest ponies, and commoners' pigs, cattle and donkeys wandering about. Other animals include foxes, stoats, badgers, and so on, and there are many species of birds to be seen. Remember, you are forbidden to feed the animals. Don't do it. If you do you'll only encourage them to stray onto roads where they might either cause accidents, or be hurt or killed themselves.
Newtownstewart: Baronscourt Forest has a good two mile long trail. You'll see deer enclosures, Japanese Sika, and a wildfowl refuge in this coniferous forest.
Nottingham: *see* Butterflies, Bees, Insects and Moths
Perth: Kinnoull Hill, not far from Perth, has a three mile nature trail which concentrates on woodland ecology. You might well see deer and red squirrels. You can get a guide at the start of the trail or from the Park and Recreation Department in Marshall Place.
Queensferry: Hopetoun House has fallow and roe deer, and St Kilda sheep.
Rugeley: *see* Information Centres
St Florence: *see* Bird Gardens
Sandringham: Go on a nature trail through the grounds of Sandringham House and see roe and fallow deer and red squirrels.
Sevenoaks: Knole Park covers 1000 acres of rich, rolling countryside, wonderful for walking and picnics – watch out, some of the deer are so tame that they'll come to share your food. Knole House is one of the largest private houses in England. Just think, there are 365 rooms, 52 staircases and 7 courtyards.
Staindrop: Raby Castle is set in a magnificent landscaped

park which has two herds of deer. You can also visit the castle and see horse-drawn carriages. Check for details of the opening of the castle.

Torridon: *see* Information Centres

Waddesdon: *see* Bird Gardens

Books

Deer, Raymond E Chaplin (Blandford)
Deer, Ralph Whitlock (Priory Press)
Deer, Alfred Leutscher (Franklin Watts)

Falconry and Birds of Prey

Birds of prey include eagles, falcons, harriers, hawks, vultures and owls. These are hunters of the air, but today they are on the decline partly because many of their natural habitats are destroyed by man, and partly because of poisoning by toxic chemicals. However, there are signs that in some places they are beginning to return.

Birds of prey are thought of as birds which eat only warm-blooded animals, and although this is often true, there are those who prefer cold-blooded creatures, and a few that are partially vegetarian. People are also inclined to think of them as very large birds but they can be almost as small as a sparrow, like the pygmy falcon. Others are indeed big – the condor might have a wing-span of ten feet. Their wings vary and the shape and size often depends on the kind of food they need. A vulture which feeds on carrion has long broad wings, for it might cover up to 200 miles a day in its search for food. Most falcons have narrow wings which enable them to fly at great speed for many of them catch their prey by chasing it. The Peregrine falcon, for example, soars high above its prey and then dives steeply, 'stooping' on its victim at a tremendous rate.

You will find that practically all birds of prey have three toes pointing forward and one backwards. They have developed this way since they are useful weapons for killing and tearing at a carcase. Those who are fish-eaters have two claws pointing in each direction so that their wriggling food can be firmly gripped. Their beaks are strong and curved so that they can be used to rip flesh, but some, like owls, prefer to eat their victims whole.

Falconry has been a sport for centuries. In Asia and the Middle East it has been practised for thousands of years, and from there gradually spread into Europe. In the Middle Ages, it became a rich man's sport. Today it has renewed popularity, but it needs patience as well as skill, and the help of an experienced falconer to learn this art.

You can see falcons and birds of prey in most zoos and many bird gardens, and there are a few places where you can see demonstrations and displays and learn something of the art of falconry.

Places to visit

Chester: Chester Zoo has a good bird of prey and owl collection.

Chilham: Chilham Castle is worth visiting for its lovely gardens and woodland walks, but there are also plenty of other things to do. There are wildfowl to watch, aviaries to walk through and the Battle of Britain Museum to examine, but best of all are the free-flying eagles and falconry displays. These take place at 15.30 every day that the garden is open – really whenever the weather is good enough.

Colwyn Bay: Welsh Mountain Zoo has lots of birds of prey and you can see first class displays of falconry. It's an interesting zoo by any standards. You'll see all the animals, birds and reptiles you'd expect to see, the penguins are visible through the new underwater observation facilities, and there's an alligator beach. You'll get a thrill, too, if you go and eat in the Treetops Restaurant – the lions are down below, perhaps looking hungrily up at you and licking their lips. The children's zoo is bound to delight the really young.

Edinburgh: Edinburgh Zoo usually has a lot of birds of prey and owls on display.

Great Witchingham: Norfolk Wildlife Park has an excellent collection of birds of prey and owls.

London: London Zoo has up to fifty species of birds of prey that come out in the day-time, and well over twenty species of owls.

Newent: Falconry Centre is the place to go to see eagles, falcons, hawks, owls and other birds. There's Hawk Walk where you can see trained birds, each jessed and leashed. There's an informative museum with falconry gear, photographs, prints, models, and quite a lot about conservation. There is also an aviary for birds of prey, and a flying ground for demonstrations and displays which take place daily, providing the weather is good enough.

Books
Birds of Prey, Glenys & Derek Lloyd (Hamlyn All Colour Paperbacks)
Birds of Prey, Ralph Whitlock (Priory Press)

Seals and Otters

All baby animals are appealing, and perhaps baby seals and baby otters are among the most attractive.

Seals
There are a number of locations around the British Isles where you might well see seals. They are curious creatures. They'll pop up quite unexpectedly to listen to music – even a tune on a penny whistle will interest them. Their bodies are well adapted to the conditions in which they live. When diving, seals close their ears and noses, but they keep their big eyes open so that they can hunt for food while under water. A fully grown seal will eat between ten and fifteen pounds of fish a day, so you can see that they have to be good hunters in order to survive.

Rocks and sandbanks are the most likely places to find seals out of the water, but there are some stretches of beaches where baby seals are found on their own. If you come across one, don't feel that you must get it back to the sea. What has happened is that the baby has probably become separated from its mother in bad weather, and has managed to reach dry land. It needs to rest. Returning it to the water too soon means that the baby animal will have to use even more of its waning strength in an effort to reach the beach again. You should immediately inform an animal rescue organization, the coast-guards or the police, leave it alone, and try to ensure that other people do the same. Putting it back in the sea really might mean that you are condemning it to death

Otters

Otters are delightful. On 1 January 1978 these lively and intelligent animals became protected in England and Wales after a long campaign to help them. In spite of this protection, otters are still in danger. Pollution is their greatest enemy. If the food they live on becomes contaminated by poisonous chemicals, they will eventually consume a lethal amount and will die. At the same time the draining of marshes and the cleaning up of river banks deprive these animals of the kind of home they need. Positive action needs to be taken to ensure that the surviving otters will continue to breed.

Organizations

The Otter Trust, Earsham, Nr Bungay, Suffolk NR35 2AF, Tel Bungay 3470, aims to promote the conservation of otters everywhere. They also want to maintain a representative collection in semi-natural but controlled conditions, both for research and interest and education, to carry out research into breeding with the aim of releasing young animals in suitable reserves, to reinforce a depleted wild population, and to promote and support field studies. Ordinary membership admits a member and a friend to the centre free of charge, brings a free illustrated Annual Report with interesting articles and an account of the Trust's work in the year, and at least two newsletters a year.

Places to visit

Practically every zoo and wildlife centre has seals and otters. Those mentioned below are particularly interesting to visit.

Dungevan: Dungevan Castle arranges boat trips from the Castle jetty when the weather permits so that you can see baby seals.
Earsham: The Otter Trust, directed by Philip Wayre, has a unique collection of otters including Freckie and Kuala, made famous in his book *The River People.* These otters live in near-natural conditions on a 23 acre site bounded by the River Waveney with three lakes and a small stream flowing through the otter breeding enclosures. There's a good collection of waterfowl and soon there will be even more aquatic birds and mammals as well as a new exhibition hall which will be concerned with the preservation of the wetlands with particular reference to the otter as its theme.
Farne Islands: This seabird sanctuary, off the Northumberland coast between Seahouses and Bamburgh Castle, has a large colony of grey seals which you can watch at low water when they are basking.
Gweek: Seal Sanctuary is a remarkable hospital for seals, dolphins, porpoises and other sea creatures that have been washed up on the coast. You can see them recovering in the five hospital pools and observe them at close quarters. You can also wander around the woodland and follow nature trails, or simply enjoy the magnificent views.
Shorwell: Yafford Mill on the Isle of Wight is a beautifully restored 18th century water mill in the middle of a small nature reserve. The Yafford seals have company in the form of rare cattle, sheep and pigs. There's a unique collection of antique farm machinery and tools, and if small children become bored, they can have a good time in the play area.
Skegness: Skegness Natureland Marine Zoo runs a seal rescue service for baby seals washed up around the coast. They hand-rear the babies, feeding them on sprats, and pop them into a small pool where visitors can see them. After about three months they are tagged and then released. Of course, there are plenty of other exibits here. Sea lions and penguins compete with the seals for attention, and the tropical house with its royal pythons, scorpions and giant snails, the pets' corner, and pools with wildfowl and tropical fish all draw interested visitors.

Books

Otters, Ralph Whitlock (Priory Press)
Seals, K M Backhouse (Arthur Baker)

Ring of Bright Water, Gavin Maxwell (Longman). A shortened version for children is *The Otter's Tale,* published by Longman.
Tarka the Otter, Henry Williamson (Bodley Head)

Safari Parks

Safari Parks are areas where herds of lions, tigers and other wild animals roam freely, and you pay to drive your car through the enclosures in which they live. If you really want to see wild animals at close quarters, then this is the way to do it. You'll find that these creatures are just like people. Some are curious and come up to have a look; others will ignore you. Monkeys might even swarm over your car.

Obviously it is essential to keep the windows of your car tightly shut, and open and soft-topped cars are not allowed. The animals are just as fierce here as they are in their natural homes, and will attack you if they think you are unprotected. If your car breaks down, you must sit tight and blow your horn until help arrives – never set foot outside the car! If you don't have a car there are usually safari mini-buses to take you through the enclosures.

Places to visit

Aviemore: Highland Wildlife Park at Kincraig is a beautiful drive-through area. *See* British and European Collections and Farms.

Balloch: Cameron Loch Lomond has bears, bison, yak and many other animals in beautiful parkland. There's also a wildfowl sanctuary, a pets' corner in a walled garden, and boating as well as other attractions.

Bewdley: West Midland Safari Park consists of nearly 200 acres of pleasantly wooded parkland with natural lakes. You can drive along tarmacked roads with zebras, lions, tigers, wolves, giraffes, monkeys and other animals roaming around their enclosures. Other attractions include an animal nursery, performing dolphins, and a pet's corner.

Blair Drummond: African Safari Park, not far from Stirling, is set in beautiful wooded parkland with a lovely curving lake. There's a comprehensive collection of animals including elephants, monkeys in their own jungle, Siberian tigers, giraffes, and so on, and there's a pets' corner too. In the summer dolphins give their usual brilliant performances, and you can go on a boat safari round the chimpanzees' island and the hippo pool. If you've got any energy left, there's always the astroglide to go on and other attractions.

Lambton: Lambton Pleasure Park near Chester-le-Street covers 200 acres with a drive-through section where lions, elephants, white rhinos, eland and other exotic animals might or might not take a fancy to you. There's also a walkabout area with more animals in fenced, moated or caged areas. There's a lot to do. Once you've visited the pets' corner you can hurtle around the new adventure playground, have a go on the astroglide, admire veteran aircraft or view the fairy-tale castle.

Prescot: Knowsley Safari Park offers you a five mile drive among free-roaming big game including lions, tigers, elephants, rhinos, and cheetahs. There's an entertaining monkey jungle, a pets' corner, and a dolphinarium.

Warminster: Longleat House has a fine safari park. You can drive over six miles of road through seven wild animal reserves – Siberian tigers, elephants, rhino, buffalo and the famous Longleat lions amongst others. By the time you've visited all the other animals, looked at the monkey jungle, been on a safari trip, enjoyed the antics of the sea lions and watched the hippos, you'll be ready for a picnic among the giraffes. There's masses more to do – fishing, animal rides, a pets' corner, miniature and model railways to admire, and a maze to get lost in.

Windsor: Royal Windsor Safari Park has large enclosures to drive through with lions, tigers, zebras, baboons, camels and other animals living in near-natural conditions. The Sea World has pools for sea lions and penguins, there are dolphins going through their routine, and a Killer Whale which you can observe through special underwater viewing facilities. For those not in cars, safari trains or buses will whip you around the park. Other attractions include a children's farm and zoo, a reptile house, a boating lake, and a really big fort.

Woburn: Woburn Wild Animal Kingdom covers 300 acres and concentrates mainly on African animals. It's one of the largest and most comprehensive reserves outside Africa. A wide variety of animals wander freely through large paddocks. There's also the jungle cabin ride to Drakeloe Lake where there's a chimpanze island and sea lions, dolphins eager to entertain you, and small animals to make friends with in the pets' corner.

Zoos, Wildlife Centres and Farms

A visit to a zoo is the ideal trip if you want to see every type of animal from all over the world. There's something for everyone, and many now have additional attractions like children's zoos, chimpanzees' tea-parties, miniature railways, and funfairs.

In recent years there has been a trend towards giving captive animals much greater freedom, and now there are a lot of wildlife parks and centres where the animals are kept in more natural conditions. What you must remember is that where there are free-roaming animals, you must never stand behind them. A startled or frightened animal may kick out or back up suddenly – and that wouldn't be much fun if you were standing behind an elephant. The other thing you must do is to obey the rules about feeding animals. Quite a lot have become sick or dangerously ill, and some have even died because stupid people have given them unsuitable food to eat.

You'll see that we have divided this into two chapters since some wildlife parks and zoos have animals from all over the world while others concentrate on British or European animals. The first chapter concentrates on general zoos and centres, the second on mainly British and European collections and farms. The farms have been included because most of them are concerned with the preservation and breeding of rare breeds of farm animals.

Organizations

Gannet Club is for junior associate members of the Royal Zoological Society of Scotland, Scottish National Zoological Park, Murrayfield, Edinburgh, Tel 031 334 9171. The Club is for those who are seriously interested in learning about and becoming involved in wildlife work. There are meetings every Saturday morning during term time, and activities include films and talks. Members receive three issues a year of the magazine *Gannet.* The club is divided into two groups – juniors who are under 12, and seniors who are over 12 years old. You can become an associate member of the Royal Zoological Society of Scotland without joining the Gannet Club. Benefits include free admission to the zoo, and special lectures and films.

Junior Zoo Club at Belfast Zoo, Hazelwood, Antrim Road, Belfast, Tel Belfast 776277 is a new club for children aged 8-14 years. Members receive a club badge, a sticker, the Zoo Club magazine, and free admission to monthly meetings.

Activities include lectures, films, quizzes, competitions, demonstrations and all kinds of projects. You can also get advice on pets.

North of England Zoological Society is based at Chester Zoo. There is no special membership for children, but if your parents belong they can get tickets to the zoo for you at half the normal price. There is a monthly magazine *Chester Zoo News* to which anyone can subscribe.

Young Zoologists' Club, the XYZ Club, is based at the London Zoo and Whipsnade. Members receive a badge, a membership card, six free tickets to the zoo, a magazine three times a year, and there is an information bureau. All sorts of things go on during the holidays – animal collecting expeditions, forums, discussions, film shows, field courses, demonstrations in animal photography – really interesting activities.

Places to visit

Alfriston: Drusillas Zoo Park really is fun to visit because there's so much to do. There's a variety of breeding groups of animals including monkeys, racoons, penguins, and rare breeds of sheep and cattle. The children's zoo, an adventure playground, carthorse and wagon rides, a vineyard, a pottery and a farm playground all make it a must for adults and toddlers alike.

Ballagh: Curraghs Wildlife Park has exotic birds and animals in walk-through aviaries and paddocks, all in a pleasantly landscaped area. Penguins, monkeys, llamas and Californian sea lions seem to be special favourites here. There's a Noah's Ark surrounded by water which is the home of some small animals and birds.

Banham: Banham Zoo and Woolly Monkey Sanctuary consists of 20 acres in rural East Anglia. It concentrates on primates and there's a splendid collection – there's the famous rare breeding group of woolly monkeys, and howlers, sakis, siamangs, spider monkeys, chimpanzees and others, all very entertaining. Bears, otters, sea lions and many other animals keep them company. You can stroll in the grounds, look at the deer park, and admire the brilliant exotic birds while you are there.

Basildon-on-Thames: Child-Beale Wildlife Trust has mammals including big cats, Highland cattle, Soay sheep, and many other species. As you stroll in the grounds and wander along riverside walks you'll see ornamental pheasants, peafowl, flamingoes and wildfowl. There's a playground for the young if they become tired of looking at the animals.

Bekesbourne: Howlett's Zoo Park is famous for its remarkable group of breeding gorillas. Indian and Siberian tigers, free-running herds of deer and antelope, African and Indian elephants, black rhinos and many other species can also be seen.

Belfast: Belfast Zoological Gardens, situated on the slopes of Cave Hill, offers you a marvellous view across Belfast Lough and the Irish Sea. The zoo is well stocked with a comprehensive collection of birds, animals and reptiles, many now housed in airy enclosures. Don't miss the impressive group of lions.

Blackpool: Blackpool Zoo Park has an interesting collection. The kangaroos hop eagerly about their new enclosure, the sea lions have fun in their very own pool, and the gibbons occupy a private island. There's a free-flight hall with bright birds zooming about tropical plants, and for the young there's an animal nursery and a children's corner.

Bristol: Bristol Zoological Gardens, set in very pleasant and spacious gardens, has all your old favourites – elephants, monkeys, Polar bears, and so on. You should especially look out for white tigers, okapi, black rhinos and the breeding group of giraffes. There's a nocturnal house, an aquarium with marine and freshwater fish, and a good collection of birds and reptiles.

Broxbourne: Although Broxbourne Zoo is comparatively new, it already has over 250 animals and birds in its 22 acres, and the collection is steadily growing. Animals include tigers, lions, puma, bears, chimpanzees, leopards, deer, and many birds of all kinds including some magnificent eagles. There's an African safari jungle – a remarkable display of glass fibre animals and monsters.

Chessington: Chessington Zoo offers non-stop entertainment, and is particularly good for the young. The grounds consist of 65 acres, so the animals aren't cooped up, and there's a comprehensive collection of animals, birds, and reptiles from all over the world. Don't forget to visit the pets' corner, the model railway, the funfair and circus, the Dinosaur Park, and the boating lake.

Chester: Chester Zoo and Gardens is the home of the North of England Zoological Society. It is rightly renowned for its excellent collection of animals, many housed in open-air enclosures in extensive gardens. There's plenty for you to do and see. You can feel the heat of the tropical house, walk through the aviary, watch the activity in the nocturnal house, shudder at the slithery reptiles, and see darting colourful fish in the aquarium. This really is a pleasant place to go for a day out. Much of the zoo can be visited by waterbus – it's an excellent way of getting about.

Cleobury Mortimer: Clee Hill Bird and Animal Gardens is a pleasant place for a day out. There are plenty of birds from all over the world, and the mammals include llamas, wallabies, deer and sheep.

Colchester: Colchester Zoo has apes, monkeys, big cats, elephants, bears, birds, reptiles, sea lions, penguins, an aquarium, and a Moonlight World, all set in a beautiful 40 acre park. The birds of prey here are especially interesting.

Colwyn Bay: *see* Falcons and Birds of Prey

Coventry: Coventry Zoo Park has a good and varied collection of animals, birds and reptiles. There are leopards, ostriches, bears, monkeys and other favourites, and best of all, the famous chimpanzees. You'll get a lot of fun out of the dolphinarium, the performing sea lions, and the children's corner.

Cricket St Thomas: West Country Wildlife Park is set in really beautiful surroundings with nine lakes and waterfalls in a lovely valley. There are large paddocks with many species of animals ranging from antelopes to zebras. There's a 2 acre walled garden with big cats, and the monkeys have plenty of room to play. You can get the feel of a tropical jungle in the walk-through aviary, while martially-minded youngsters can command the children's fort.

Cromer: Cromer Zoo is very pleasantly situated – some of its inhabitants even have a view of the sea. These well-housed animals include bears, monkeys, wallabies, and camels, and the reptiles and birds are well represented.

Dervock: Causeway Coast Lion Park has two lion enclosures and other exotic species of African wildlife including zebras, ostriches, and its own monkey jungle. There's a zoo for children and many of its appealing inhabitants can be freely handled. The curio shop has examples of genuine African handicrafts.

Downend: Robin Hill Country Park and Zoological Park covers

80 acres of woodland and downland on the Isle of Wight, and has a good collection of mammals, birds and insects. There's an indoor tropical jungle house with reptiles, insects and birds, pony and donkey rides, 10 acre walk-through animal enclosures, a nature trail, a playground, and for anyone who has still got any energy after enjoying all that lot, there's a Commando-style assault course.

Dudley: Dudley Zoo is in the grounds of Dudley Castle. The terrain is wooded and hilly, and so the animals have interesting surroundings. The bears, lions and tigers, for instance, live in specially adapted quarries. This zoo has bred Arabian gazelles, Polar bears and apes. Make sure that you see the reptile house, the British wildlife collection, and the aquarium.

Edinburgh: Edinburgh Zoo, the headquarters of the Royal Zoological Society of Scotland, has a comprehensive collection. In fact, every animal you would expect to see is likely to be found there. The aquarium is excellent. There are reptile and ape houses, a parrot garden, and a children's zoo. If the weather is fine you'll find the chimpanzees are having tea at 15.00. This zoo is particularly famous for its Antarctic penguins, so don't miss them.

Exmouth: Sandy Bay Leisure Complex, recently enlarged, has interesting animals including some rare breeds like the Vietnamese pot-bellied pigs, and there are lots of small mammals such as African bush-babies, coatis, and mongooses. There's a wide variety of birds as well some larger animals.

Fazely: Drayton Manor Park and Zoo is set in 160 acres of wooded parkland with lakes and pleasant walks. The zoo itself occupies 15 acres and houses a variety of animals, reptiles and birds. There are lions, leopards, puma, a large colony of monkeys, crocodiles, bird paddocks, and a farm section. You can set off on a jungle cruise, chug around on the miniature railway, swing high on a cable car or have fun in the amusement park.

Glasgow: Calderpark Zoo has a really comprehensive collection of mammals, reptiles, fish and birds, with many of its inhabitants now living in new airy enclosures. This zoo concentrates on breeding, so you can hope to see some baby animals when you come on a visit. It also runs a special educational service.

Gorey: Jersey Zoological Park, founded by Gerald Durrell, the author of many amusing books, is famous as the headquarters of the Jersey Wildlife Preservation Trust. It has had tremendous success in breeding rare species like Lowland gorillas, the spectacled bear, and white-eared pheasants. This zoo is both entertaining and instructive with a very pleasant atmosphere.

Heathfield: Heathfield Wildlife Park keeps its animals in a really super setting. There are a lot of them, many roaming freely, and you can visit Bird City and fuss over farmyard pets. If you happen to be keen on old cars, then there's a bonus. *Chitty Chitty Bang Bang* and other notable cars are there, and for those who enjoy bygones, there's a museum of agricultural archaeology to wander around.

Kessingland: Suffolk Wildlife and Country Park has a good general collection of animals including big cats and monkeys. There's a reptile house, a pets' corner, and the birds include eagles, parrots, waterfowl, owls, vultures, macaws and cockatoos. It's very pleasant with wooded slopes, marshland, ponds and a lake. Keen fishermen should go. You can fish in the river during the season at no extra charge.

Knaresborough: Knaresborough Zoological Gardens are in the grounds of Conyingham House. The big cats are especially well represented – lions, tigers, black panthers, pumas and others. There are plenty of other animals to admire and you can see the sea lions fed. The animal and snake handling exhibitions are fascinating. They take place twice a day from Easter to September providing the weather is good enough. Take your camera with you. You should get a spectacular snap.

Linton: New Linton Zoological Gardens has had considerable success in breeding animals, and its collection includes big cats, bears, wolves, llamas and many other animals, all housed in landscaped enclosures. This is a place where you'll almost certainly see a number of baby animals.

London: Battersea Park Zoo has both exotic and familiar animals, carefully selected with young children in mind. On fine days there are usually pony rides or rides in pony traps.

London: Crystal Palace Zoo keeps on growing, but it's still a comparatively small zoo for small children. The animals tend to be small too – Shetland and Welsh ponies, monkeys, otters and deer. The birds are usually exotic and entertaining.

London: London Zoo, opened in 1828, is enormous. There are about 1500 species and this means that over 8000 mouths have to be fed each day. Many of the animals have been rehoused recently – the lions, for instance, have new terraces. The walk-through Snowdon aviary is impressive, and the Moonlit World of nocturnal animals is fascinating. These creatures are usually awake when we are asleep, but night and day have been reversed for them, so you can see them going about their business in the day time. Other attractions include the children's zoo with ever-popular rides for young children, the chimpanzees' tea-party at the Clock Tower, and the zoo bus, a waterbus that starts from Little Venice. It's a nice way to arrive.

Looe: Monkey Sanctuary is the home of a large breeding colony of the rare Amazon woolly monkey. You can watch them having a good time in the trees and meet them in the grounds. There are talks and discussions each morning and afternoon, and these are given indoors whenever the weather is wet, cold or windy. It's much wiser to take young children only on a fine day.

Lympne: Port Lympne Wildlife Sanctuary has a superb collection of rare and beautiful animals living in 270 acres of grass paddocks and woodland. Not only will you see truly magnificent specimens collected from all over the world, but you'll find yourself in a lovely place which offers stunning views.

Margate: Dreamland Park Zoo has a varied collection of animals, birds in walk-through aviaries, and reptiles and other exhibits. The favourite still seems to be Old MacDonald's Farm with farmyard animals and domestic pets.

Newport, Essex: Mole Hall Wildlife Park is based on an Elizabethan house surrounded by a moat crossed by four bridges – an impressive start to a visit. There's a good collection of animals and birds in enclosures and pools. It's particularly strong on primates, and the Canadian otters and the marsupials are worth looking out for.

Newport, Gwent: Whitson Zoological Park is set in the magnificent grounds of an 18th century house. You'll find bears, monkeys, baboons, and many reptiles and birds among the inhabitants. The aquarium is actually in the cellars of the house.

Newquay: Newquay Zoo is an open-plan zoo, well-landscaped, and with large paddocks for the animals. Birds flash around in the walk-through aviary, sea lions show off in their own pool, and there is a tropical house, bear pits, a monkey walk, four lakes with pelicans, flamingoes and penguins, and a pets' corner.

Paignton: Paignton Zoo occupies about 100 acres of really lovely gardens. It has a tropical and subtropical house, and a collection of animals, birds and reptiles from all over the world. You'll see Lar gibbons on their island in the lake, and baboons playing about on their rock. The aquarium with its flashing, brilliantly coloured fish is well worth a visit.
Poole: Poole Park Zoo has parrots and other tropical birds, leopards, pumas, a monkey house, tropical house, children's zoo, and other animals. Although not large, it is well-organized and a very pleasant place to visit.
Rampton: Sundown Pets' Garden has pet and farm animals, large play areas and a toy jungle.
Scarborough: *see* Aquaria and Dolphinaria
Skegness: *see* Seals and Otters
Southam: Southam Wildlife Park is set in 7 acres and has an interesting collection of animals with tigers, pumas, bears, panthers, chimpanzees and monkeys among others. There are exotic and tropical birds, birds of prey and waterfowl. Don't be surprised if a chimpanzee takes it into his head to guide you around the children's corner. At times there are special displays of lions in an open arena. This zoo is always willing to give advice and help on animals and birds.
Southampton: Southampton Zoo is not one of the larger zoos, but with its gardens bright with flowers and a generally pleasant atmosphere, it's always worth visiting. There's a comprehensive collection of animals, lots of birds in the aviaries, and the sea lions obviously enjoy seeing the visitors as much as the visitors enjoy looking at them.
Southport: Southport Zoo is another of the smaller zoos, but there's an interesting collection of animals. There's a rare breeding group of mandrills, and breeding chimpanzees and lions. Along with the other animals there are duck and flamingo pools, aviaries, a reptile house, and an alligator beach.
Tenby: St Catherine's Island Zoo is fun to get to. It's on a small island fortress off the beach at Tenby, and you can only cross at low tide. The zoo is noted for its entertaining group of Macaque monkeys and cockatoo monkeys besides a representative collection of other animals and birds. Small children will want to head for the pets' corner.
Thetford: Kilverstone Wild Life Park and Falabella Horse Stud is sometimes known as the South American Zoo since it

specializes in Central and South American birds and animals – bison, jaguar, alpaca monkeys, macaws and parrots are just a few of its residents. There's a pets' corner, a deer park, a riverside walk, and an adventure playground. Everyone will love the miniature Falabella horses from the Argentine.
Twycross: Twycross Zoo has a varied collection for you to admire, and there's also a reptile house, a pets' corner, a children's playground, and in the summer there are donkey rides and a miniature railway in operation.
Whipsnade: Whipsnade Zoo is used as a country home for many of the animals from the London Zoo, and it houses over 2000 animals in its 500 acre park, all kept in as near-natural surroundings as possible. You can see rare species like the herd of Père David deer and Przewalski's wild horses. There is so much to see – elephants, primates, big cats, camels, giraffes and many other species. There are dolphins and other water mammals to be seen through the new underwater viewing facilities, and small children can look forward to camel or pony rides, or a drive in a llama cart. This zoo is so successful that over 80 per cent of its mammals have been born here. There are various ways of getting around. You can drive in your own car, take the zoo motor train in summer, or ride on a steam railway through the famous white rhino enclosure.
Winchester: Marwell Zoological Park, only opened in 1972, now houses a major wild animal collection in its 200 acres. The enclosures are as natural as possible and the animals are grouped according to their continent of origin. It not only has all the animals you would expect to find in a well-stocked zoo, but there are rare ones too – the large breeding group of scimitar-horned oryx, for instance. The new ape enclosure is splendid, there are waterfowl gardens, a children's zoo and a playground.

British and European Collections and Farms

Places to visit
Ardfern: Lunga Wildlife Reserve is the place to go for Scottish fauna and birds, all in very pleasant woodland and marshland.

Bickleigh: Bickleigh Mill Farm consists of traditional stone and timber buildings in the Exe valley. You'll see Devon farming and country life as it used to be at the turn of the century. There are Shire horses, some rare breeds of goats, sheep, pigs, rabbits and others, and you can watch the birds who live on Duck Island.

Birmingham: Cannon Hill Nature Centre displays living animals of the British Isles and Europe in both outdoor and indoor enclosures. You can see lynx, foxes, badgers, polecats, owls and many others.

Bridgerule: Furze Farm Park, set in 26 acres, has farm animals of many breeds, a farming through the ages display, a blacksmith's and a wheelwright's, a nature trail and other attractions.

Chillingham: Chillingham Wild Cattle are unique. This herd of about fifty animals are the sole survivors of their species. It is known that they have lived here for about 700 years, but many think that they roamed prehistoric Northumbria. Although some visitors think that they are not very different from domesti cattle, they should be aware that under certain circumstances they can be dangerous.

Coulby Newham: Newham Grange Leisure Farm features rare breeds of farm animals. There's an interpretive centre, an audio-visual display, an agricultural museum, and farm and nature trails.

Dalkeith: Dalkeith Palace and Park has signposted nature trails. See if you can spot roe deer, red squirrels, foxes and other small animals, and see how many species of birds you can identify.

Dedham: Vale of Dedham Heavy Horse Centre has marvellous Suffolk punches and Shire horses. There are wagon rides, demonstrations of blacksmithing, musical drives and other attractions.

Elsham: Elsham Hall Country Park has domestic animals, a bird sanctuary, nature trails with country quizzes, and you can go on trails with wardens.

Farway: Farway Country Park, near Colyton, has a collection of rare breeds and farm animals living in over 130 acres of countryside overlooking the Colne valley. Young children can enjoy pony and donkey rides and rides in horse-drawn wagons. The disabled are admitted free.

Fletchers Bridge: Bodmin Farm Park is a working stock farm with both familiar and unfamiliar animals. There's a pets' corner, pony rides, a play area, and old farming implements to see.

Glasgow: Linn Park which consists of over 200 acres of woodland has a collection of Highland cattle and British ponies, a children's zoo and an excellent nature trail which will help you to notice insects which you would normally overlook, as well as flowers and trees to enjoy.

Great Witchingham: Norfolk Wildlife Park, created by Philip Wayre, houses Europe's largest collection of European mammals. These are exhibited in open enclosures in natural surroundings. There are bears, wolves, lynx, alpine ibex and many others to watch. There are two walk-through aviaries as well as wildfowl and birds of prey. This park, the headquarters of the Pheasant Trust, has already bred more than 1000 birds of endangered species. It is hoped that visitors will begin to understand the importance of conserving European wildlife.

Guiting Power: Cotswold Farm Park has succeeded in preserving rare breeds of British livestock. These fascinating animals are exhibited in ditched rather than fenced enclosures. There's a farm trail, an indoor study centre, illustrated talks showing films on rare breeds, and for younger visitors, pets and baby animals, pony and trap rides, and an adventure playground.

Ipsden: *see* Bird Gardens

Kincraig: Highland Wildlife Park has breeding groups in a splendid Highland setting. There's a drive-through section where you can observe red deer, Highland cattle, bison and other animals wandering about, and you'll see about another sixty species of animals in the grounds. Look in at the aviaries, and don't miss the extremely informative 'Man and Fauna in the Highlands' exhibition.

Lilford: Lilford Park has a wide selection of farm animals and birds. You can enjoy the children's farm and the adventure playground. There are special events here from March to October.

Llandyssul: West Wales Farm Park has many different kinds of pigs, sheep and fowl, all of them rare breeds.

Lowther: Wildlife and Country Park has British and European species. Residents include otters, badgers, wild pigs, rare breeds of cattle, goats and sheep. There's a play area for young children.

Mablethorpe: Mablethorpe Animal and Bird Gardens has small animals, donkeys, an aviary, parrots and a butterfly display.

Maidenhead Thicket: Courage Shire Horse Centre has superb Shire horses on show as well as game birds and small animals to fuss over. Dray rides are given at weekends if the weather is good enough, and other attractions include traction engines and farm equipment.
Matlock: Riber Castle Fauna Reserve covers 20 acres and contains a very good collection of British and European birds and mammals, many of them like pine martens and polecats seldom seen. These and rare breeds of farm animals are kept in near-natural conditions. You can also visit domestic animals, a butterfly exhibition, models of prehistoric animals, vintage cars, a model railway and a playground.
Palacerigg: Palacerigg Country Park, less than 3 miles from Cumbernauld, has a wide variety of wildlife. Try and spot deer, foxes, stoats, badgers and weasels. In the paddocks you'll find mink, wolves and wild cats. There's a nature centre, but this is closed on Mondays. A museum is opening soon, and that should offer even more interest to those already keen on nature.
St Florence: *see* Bird Gardens
Sparkwell: Dartmoor Wildlife Park is set in beautiful countryside on the edge of Dartmoor. Over 100 species of animals and birds live in 25 acres of near-natural surroundings. There are many European mammals, reptiles and birds breeding here, and you can meet some of the more friendly birds and animals in a special 2 acre enclosure. There's a special viewing tower so that you can observe six species of deer.
Skeyton: Skeyton Farm Park concentrates on rare and old breeds of livestock – cattle, horses, pigs, poultry, sheep and other animals and birds.
Tighnabruaich: Tighnabruaich Wildlife Centre has roedeer, blue hares, ducks and many other animals and birds. The photo-safari hides make observation even more interesting.
Wemworthy: Ashley Countryside Collection has twenty-five rare breeds of sheep and a unique fleeces exhibition. You can also see old farm and farmhouse equipment.
Weyhill: Weyhill European Wildlife Park has a very good collection of animals and birds. You'll see deer, sheep, badgers, stoats, foxes, wolves, wildcat and others. European birds of prey, waterfowl and reptiles are there too. You can see the wildlife and countryside museum, and follow a nature trail.

Wickham Market: Easton Farm Park is a unique country park based on a working farm on the banks of the River Deben. You'll see plenty of farm animals, some rare and some familiar, a Victorian dairy, a modern milking parlour, a beekeeping exhibition, a pets' paddock, a nature trail, and other attractions which are bound to interest the whole family. On Sundays throughout the season there are demonstrations of crafts like corn dolly making and spinning.

Pondlife

This book is full of places where you can go and see wildlife but unless you live near them, a visit does mean going on buses, trains or getting your parents to take you there by car. If you want to explore and discover wildlife on your own, most people – except those of you who live right in the middle of big cities – will have a pond fairly near their home, either in the local park, nearby woods or even in their own gardens. It might look small and dirty – but you'll be surprised how much wildlife you will find.

For a start you will almost certainly find some green, slimy stuff called algae, which is in fact masses of minute plants. And if there is algae, tiny animals will appear to feed on it, such as the water flea, called daphnia – and then insects like beetles, water boatmen and dragon-fly larvae will come to feed on the daphnia. There may be frogs – it's great fun to look for frog-spawn in the spring and watch it turn first into tadpoles and then into frogs – newts, snails, even sticklebacks and freshwater shrimps.

If the pond is a large one there may be birds nesting in the reeds and rushes around the edge. You might see mallard, tufted or pochard ducks, moorhens, coots or dabchicks – a hidden spot by the edge of the pond is a good place to watch them as sooner or later they must come to drink or feed.

Remember to wear your Wellingtons, and take with you a net and a jam-jar in which to put your 'finds', and you'll find you could easily spend a whole day at your local pond.

Books
The Ecology of Pond Life, Alfred Leutscher (Franklin Watts)
Exploring the Pond, Leslie Jackman (Evans)
The Observer's Book of Pond Life, John Clegg (Warne)
Pond and Stream Life, J Clegg (Blandford)
Pond Life – Black's Young Naturalist's Series (A & C Black)
The Young Specialist Looks at Pond Life, W Englehardt (Burke)

Wildlife in your Garden

Many creatures do still live in our cities and large towns. Parks and public gardens, cemeteries and graveyards, reservoirs and sewage farms, rubbish dumps and railway embankments all provide shelter for them. Nevertheless, as small areas of waste land are flattened by bulldozers so that houses and flats can be built, and garages and drives replace front gardens, so it becomes harder for wildlife to survive.

You can help by encouraging wildlife in your garden – after all, these creatures need only a quiet habitat, food and water. However, first of all you'll have to persuade your parents to leave a small patch of garden uncultivated, to leave the foot

of the hedge untidy, and perhaps to plant a few berry-bearing shrubs. Wild plants will attract various kinds of insects who will attract others creatures which, in their turn, eat the insects. Long grass, leaves which have collected at the foot of a hedge, or a compost heap will provide cover, and those berry-bearing shrubs will provide food.

Badgers

Although we always think of badgers living in the country, there have been many reports of them moving into the suburbs.

Badgers are really attractive mammals. They have long, strong, barrel-shaped bodies which are about three feet long. They have short, powerful legs which make them good diggers, and short, blunt tails. Their coats appear silver-grey, but actually the stiff, coarse hairs are whitish with black bands near the tips. Their legs and bellies are black, and their heads are white with black stripes running down over each ear and eye.

Badgers live in setts, underground homes with several rooms and tunnels, and more than one entrance. Both males and females are house-proud animals who constantly turf out old bedding and drag in fresh grass, bracken and dry leaves to make a new bed. They mate from February to October, but the cubs are born in February. They live with their parents until autumn or sometimes throughout the winter, and then they are turned out to fend for themselves. As you know, badgers are nocturnal animals, so unless you are very lucky, you are most unlikely to see them until after sunset.

Once it is dark, badgers amble off, following ancient tracks, foraging for food. They'll eat almost anything – earthworms, moles, frogs, snails, grass, windfall apples, blackberries, and so on. If you are lucky to have badgers in your garden, try feeding them on bread and treacle, or flaked maize and treacle – you'll have friends for life.

Birds

If you enjoy watching birds, then a small bird-table will attract many different species. There's no need to have an elaborate one, but a little roof is helpful in preventing the food from being soaked. If you don't want to go to the trouble of constructing a proper table, then why not hang an old wooden tray from a tree, or just nail it onto a post. You can also string lumps of suet, cheese and bits of fat together, and hang them on a branch. Do remember that some birds, like the song thrush, feed only on the ground, so scatter some food for them but make sure it's well away from thick cover that could be sheltering a hungry cat. Birds shouldn't be fed from April to September since if the parents take it back to the nest for nestlings, it could actually harm them, because the babies need natural food. Moving the feeding place around occasionally is a good idea, as this avoids the risk of disease.

Most people put out crumbs, and this is fine, but it's best to soak white bread first. Bones, fat, cheese, dry porridge oats, sunflower seeds, nuts (but not salted ones), apples, dried fruit, and bacon rind are all foods that will bring birds flocking to your garden. Best of all is to give the birds a chance of gathering natural food. Berry-bearing shrubs like hawthorn, elder, holly, honeysuckle, cotoneaster, flowering currant and rowan will all help birds to survive the winter. Weeds in your wild patch such as thistles, groundsel, chickweed, field poppies and ragwort will also provide food.

Grass-snakes

Grass-snakes are not poisonous, but if they are alarmed they will hiss and appear very dangerous, but then they will slither away. They are beautiful creatures with olive-brown upper bodies with vertical bars along the flanks, and two yellowish or orange-brown patches of colour on the nape of the neck followed by two black triangles. The males are about two feet long, and the females up to a foot longer.

Grass-snakes are marvellously graceful swimmers, and they eat fish, frogs, toads and newts. You will see them near ponds, in ditches and streams, or sometimes in hedgerows or along the sides of fields. They hibernate from October to March, when they sleep in piles of leaves, in ditches or holes in the ground provided there is some cover, under logs, or they tuck themselves deep into clefts in rocks. If you have a pond in your garden without goldfish, then a grass snake should be a welcome visitor, but if you do have fish — well, watch out!

Hedgehogs

Hedgehogs should be welcomed by all gardeners since they feed mainly on insects, slugs and snails. These grey-brown animals have yellow-tipped spines on their backs and sides. These are usually flat, but they spring upright when the animals protect themselves by rolling into balls.

Hedgehogs mate between March and July, so you could hope to see babies from May to September, although you won't see them in daylight since they are nocturnal animals who only shuffle off hunting after dusk. They can make a tremendous noise as they wander about, snorting and breathing loudly, so don't be alarmed if you think you hear an elephant trampling through your garden at night. Actually they are very friendly animals who are always keen to have a drink of milk. They do have very sharp ears, but they are a bit short-sighted and might easily mistake your finger for a piece of wood or even something to eat.

Hedgehogs hibernate in the winter, making themselves a kind of nest of leaves and bits of moss to keep themselves warm, so they do need dense cover, or an old hedge or a rubbish dump where they can safely tuck themselves away.

Lacewings

These slender insects get their name because of the lacework of veins on their large green wings. You'll see them in woods or small copses, but you'll also see them in hedges and gardens, flying very slowly and a bit clumsily, eating greenfly and other garden pests. They are a lovely pale green, golden-eyed, and grow up to two inches long. The eggs are laid on the end of short stalks or leaves where aphids are congregating. The larvae feed on the aphids and when fully grown, they spin a cocoon and pupate inside it. These cocoons can be spotted on bark or leaves. Later, in the summer, the adults hatch out and these too feed on aphids. Lacewings are masters of camouflage, for after eating the aphids, they press the skins onto their backs, so that they shrivel, looking like tiny bits of rubbish.

Ladybirds

Did you know that there are over forty different species of ladybirds in Britain? The most common species grow from one eighth to half an inch long, and have red or yellow bodies with black spots. In spring they fly to plants which are infested with aphids and lay their eggs. A week later these eggs have turned into grubs, and three to six weeks after that, they turn into pupae. Seven days later, they emerge as beetles.

Ladybirds hibernate in large colonies during the winter, often under loose bark or in cavities. Since they eat aphids, mealy-bugs, scale-insects and mites, you should be delighted to find them in your garden.

Shrews

There are five different species in the British Isles. You are most likely to see pygmy shrews. These small animals are just about two inches long with a tail about two thirds the length of the body, and with long snouts. Their coat is greyish-brown on the upper part, and white below. They need ground cover and tend to live in woods, in long grass, or in hedgerows, where they make long tunnels or, being a bit lazier than other species, look for an old tunnel to use.

The common shrew is slightly larger with dark brown fur on its upper body, white below, and pale brown on the flanks. They mate from spring to summer, and the litters of young are born in balls of woven grass.

These little animals feed on beetles, caterpillars, spiders, flies, earthworms and woodlice. As you know, a woman who is noisy and quarrelsome is sometimes described as a shrew. That's because that is the way that these aggressive little creatures behave, screaming at anyone who invades their territory, and chattering at nothing.

Slow-worms

Slow-worms, sometimes called blind-worms, are sometimes mistaken for snakes, but actually they belong to the lizard family, even though they have no legs. The head is similar to that of a lizard. It has ear openings, a fleshy tongue and, unlike the snake, eyelids that open and close. The body is scaled, the colour varying from grey to a creamy colour and bronze. If there is a darker stripe along the back, then it will be a female. The slow-worm grows up to eighteen inches in length. It is like other lizards in that, if grabbed by the tail, it can break off the piece that has been seized, and make its escape. However, like snakes and unlike other lizards, it also sheds its skin in one piece. The young are born in late summer, and there could be up to twenty of them.

They are useful creatures in a garden since they feed on slugs and snails and earthworms. You'll find them living in dampish areas in piles of leaf mould under hedges or the borders of copses, in rubbish dumps, compost heaps or other quiet places.

Voles

Although voles are relatives of mice and rats, they look different. The short-tailed vole grows up to four inches long, has a blunt snout, a short tail, and very small ears. Its coat varies from yellowish-brown to chocolate colour on the upper body, while below it is grey. It lives in hedgerows or rough grass, and can also be found in marshland, moorland, or in young plantations of trees where they can do quite a lot of damage by eating young shoots. However, they feed mainly on grass. They breed from March to September, and the litters are born in nests built under tufts of grass, old logs or fallen trees.

Books

How to Watch Wildlife, Gordon Burness (Studio Vista)
The Junior Naturalist's Handbook, Geoffrey G Watson (A & C Black)
Looking at Nature, Elsie Proctor (A & C Black)

Teach Yourself Watching Wildlife, Richard Philips (Knight Books)
The Young Naturalist's Handbook, Leonard Moore (Hamlyn)
There are several good series of natural history guides. Among these are Blandford Colour Guides, Black's Young Naturalist series and Collins Field Guides.

Conservation

We all know that there are serious problems of conservation and pollution and that these exist all over the world, not just in this country. Many species of birds, fishes and animals are in danger of extinction; oil spillages at sea pollute beaches, destroy birds and do untold harm to fish and crustaceans; common wild flowers disappear and forests are destroyed and not replanted – even the very air we breathe can be harmful.

Although legislation is passed to try and improve the conditions in which we live and to decrease the amount of pollution, this is not enough, and neither is it enough to agree that pollution is bad and conservation good. It is essential to take action. Why not join one of the societies below and do something positive to improve our environment and to help endangered species of birds and animals?

Organizations
The Ark Club, organized jointly by the Jersey Wildlife Preservation Trust, Les Augres Manor, Trinity, Jersey and the Wildlife Youth Service, Wallington, Surrey is for anyone under the age of 18. The club was set up by the famous naturalist Gerald Durrell, who has established a sanctuary where colonies of threatened animals live and breed in peace. As the numbers of these animals grow, they are returned to the wild to re-popula the areas from where they have vanished. Ark Club members receive a membership card and badge, free admittance to the Jersey Zoo at any time when the park is open to the public, newsletters from Gerald Durell, and four issues of *Wildlife Youth Service News* a year.
British Trust for Conservation Volunteers, Zoological Gardens, Regents Park, London SW1, Tel 01 722 7122 is the governing

body to which all members of local conservation corps are affiliated. It will advise you of conservation groups in your area, but you have to be 16 before you can actually join a party. The work the corps does is varied. You might find yourself cleaning out a pond, building a stone wall, or learning to hedge and ditch. It's all work that has to be done to preserve the countryside, and although it's often pretty tough, it's very rewarding. Sometimes these work parties last for a week or more, and then you might find yourself sleeping in a village hall or an old mill or even in a stately home. Members of the trust receive the quarterly newsletter *The Conserver* which contains articles on practical conservation work and news of all the trust's developments.

Cambient, 1 Brookside, Cambridge CB2 1JF, run by Cambridgeshire and Isle of Ely Naturalists' Trust cares for Cambridgeshire wildlife. Become a junior member and help the society to set up, protect and manage nature reserves all over the country. You'll get regular newsletters which will keep you up-to-date with local wildlife news, and you'll be able to play an active part in conservation.

Fauna Preservation Society, Zoological Gardens, Regent's Park, London NW1, Tel 01 586 0872 aims to save endangered wildlife all over the world, and works closely with the World Wildlife Fund. There's no special junior membership, but full membership means that you'll be able to go along to regular meetings and take part in the society's activities, and you'll receive *Oryx,* the society's magazine, three times a year. The society has been in existence for seventy-five years. Try and read *The Penitent Butchers* by Richard Fitter, the Secretary, and learn about its formation, development and the work it has done.

Society for the Promotion of Nature Conservation, 22 The Green, Nettleham, Lincoln is keen to welcome new members. Its magazine *Conservation Review* giving news of the society's activities will drop through your letterbox twice a year.

Watch, 22 The Green, Nettleham, Lincoln, sponsored by *The Sunday Times* and the Society for the Promotion of Nature Conservation, is a club directly concerned with the environment. Members receive a membership book, a jeans sticker, a local events diary, and the club magazine *Watchword.* Members and their families take part in an astonishingly wide variety of

projects concerned with the environment.
Wildfowl Trust *see* Birds in the Wild
Wildlife Youth Service, Wildlife, 98/106 Manor Road, Wallington, Surrey, provides money to rescue animals threatened with extinction like the cheetah and the polar bear. So many are now in danger that very determined efforts are needed to save them. There are two sections of membership. Wildlife Observers are people aged 11-18, whilst members of the Panda Club are aged 5-10. Your annual subscription will really help, and you'll get a lot of pleasure from the activities that go on – study projects, film shows, field rambles and adventure camp holidays. **Animals in Danger** is another group associated with the Wildlife Youth Service. AID has been formed to do the vital work of raising the money so desperately needed to save wildlife all over the world. They don't want you to sacrifice your pocket money, but they do need your energy, enthusiasm and ingenuity to plan and organize fund-raising events. There is no membership fee, but you can buy an AID badge – the money goes towards the fund.

Books
Animal Wildlife in Danger, D Smith and D Newton (Longman Young Books)
Conservation, James Whinray (A & C Black)
Conservation of Nature, Eric Duffey (Collins)
Conservation Scene, Geoffrey Young (Peacock Books)
The Penitent Butchers, Richard Fitter (Collins).
The Forestry Commission publish a booklet called *Wildlife Conservation in Woodlands.* (Available from booksellers or HMSO offices.)
Wildlife in Danger, Jean Mellanby (Wayland)

Forests and Parks

Britain's woodlands cover only eight per cent of the country, but they do provide areas of peace and beauty for all of us to enjoy. In order to protect wildlife and to preserve the country-side everyone must remember and follow the country code.

There are ten important points to learn, and they are all based on common sense. Remember:

1 Be careful not to start a fire.
2 Fasten all gates.
3 Keep dogs under proper control.
4 Keep to paths across farm land.
5 Don't damage fences, hedges or walls.
6 Don't leave litter – take it home.
7 Don't pollute water – it might be the water supply for thousands of people.
8 Go carefully on country roads.
9 Protect wildlife, plants and trees.
10 Respect the life of the countryside.

The Forestry Commission, 25 Saville Row, London W1 is responsible for forest land.
The Countryside Commission, John Dower House, Crescent Place, Cheltenham, Gloucestershire is responsible for National and Country Parks.

Forests
The Forestry Commission has a far greater effect on our lives than most people realize. It owns over three million acres of land and although its main function is to produce timber, the Commission now places much greater emphasis on recreational facilities than before. It looks after seven forest parks in Britain, four in Scotland, one on the Border, and it also manages the New Forest.

Most people who enjoy our forests also like peace and quiet and so, on the whole, visitors must leave their cars in parks at the entrances to forests, although recently several miles of scenic drives have been opened.

To help everyone to get the most out of the forest, over 400 forest walks and trails have been signposted, and a number of Visitors Centres opened, as you will see under Information Centres and Nature Trails.

In some places there are observation towers for keen naturalists, and you can get day permits to fish, or go orienteering, riding, pony-trekking, sailing, canoeing, and watch car rallying. You can camp on some sites and even rent cabins and other accommodation for holidays. A new interest has grown up in Thetford Forest. This is backpacking, a tougher form of camping where the sites provided are wild and isolated and where the only facility is water. This has proved so popular that the Commission is considering organizing backpacking in other forests.

The Forestry Commission publishes free pamphlets called *See Your Forests* and these give details of all the forest walks and trails together with other recreational facilities. These are available for Northern England, Southern England, Scotland and Wales.

National Parks

There are ten national parks in England and Wales, and free leaflets about each can be obtained from the Countryside Commission. Most of the land is privately owned, and people live and work on it, so you must observe the rights of access and follow the country code. Each of the parks has Information Centres and you can get information from HMSO booklets.
Brecon Beacons: National Park Information Officer, 6 Glamorgan Street, Brecon, Tel Brecon 2763.
Dartmoor: Dartmoor National Park Authority, County Hall, Topsham Road, Exeter, Tel Exeter 77977.
Exmoor: Exmoor National Park Department, Exmoor House, Dulverton, Somerset, Tel Dulverton 665.
Lake District: Lake District National Park Office, County Hall, Kendal, Tel Kendal 24555.
North Yorks Moors: North York Moors National Park Information Service, The Old Vicarage, Bondgate, Helmsley, North Yorkshire, Tel Bondgate 657.
Northumberland: National Park Office, Bede House, All Saints Centre, Newcastle upon Tyne, Tel Newcastle upon Tyne 610796.
Pembrokeshire: Pembrokeshire National Park Office, County Offices, Haverfordwest, Dyfed, Tel Haverfordwest 3131.
Snowdonia: Snowdonia National Park, Yr Hen Ysgol, Maentwrog Blaenau Ffestiniog, Gwynedd.
Yorkshire Dales: Yorkshire Dales National Park Information Service, Colvend, Hebden Road, Grassington, Skipton, Yorkshire, Tel Grassington 752748.

Peak District: Peak National Park Office, Baslow Road, Bakewell, Derbyshire, Tel Bakewell 2881.

Country Parks

A country park isn't a wild, remote area on the scale of national parks. Most country parks are small secluded areas of woodlands or open parkland where country lovers can study natural history or simply enjoy the peace and beauty of the countryside. Some parks have places where you can fish, sail or ride, and others have picnic areas, information centres and other facilities. The Countryside Commission now recognizes more than 100 country parks and publishes a complete list with details of where they are and what facilities are available.

Books

British Trees in Colour, Cyril Hart & Charles Raymond (Michael Joseph)
A Colour Guide to Familiar Trees, Leaves, Bark and Fruit, Jaromir Pokorny (Octopus)
The Observer's Book of Trees, Herbert L Edlin (Warne)
Plant Communities, Anne Bülow-Olsen (Penguin Nature Series)
The Young Specialist Looks at Trees, Alois Kosch (Burke)

Holidays

If you are passionately interested in bird-watching or in natural history generally, what better way to spend your holiday than going on a course specially organized for people of similar interests? If you already belong to a society which organizes holidays for its members, then it is probably best (and cheapest) to go on one of those. But if you don't belong to such a society, or feel like a change, why not try one of these listed below? Write in good time to the address given, asking for information and enclosing a stamped, addressed envelope for the reply.

Holiday Centres

Birds for All Seasons, 7-8 Stratford Place, London W1, Tel 01 629 6618. Bird-watching weekends. Age 10+.
Churchtown Farm Field Studies Centre, Lanlivery, Bodmin, Cornwall, Tel Lostwithiel 872148. One week bird-watching

holidays. Handicapped children particularly welcome with their families.

Isles of Scilly Wildlife Holidays, Pendbrose, St Mary's has 7-14 day bird-watching holidays. Beginners are taken from March-early October. Age 16+.

Juniper Hill Field Centre, Warden, Dorking, Surrey, Tel Dorking 3849 has long weekends for bird-watchers. Age 13+.

Larpool Hall Activity and Field Centre, Director, Larpool Drive, Larpool Lane, Whitby, Yorkshire, Tel Whitby 2737 has 7 day holidays which include natural history. Age: 8-14.

Malham Tarn Field Centre, Warden, Settle, North Yorkshire Tel Airton 331, has 4-7 day bird-watching holidays at various times of the year. Age: 13+.

Medina Valley Field Centre, Secretary, Dodnor Lane, Newport, Isle of Wight Tel Newport 2195 has weekend or 7 day courses in a wide range of field study topics from bird migration to marine biology. It also organizes bird-watching expeditions to Norway in August. Age: 14+ (12 if accompanied).

Mountain and Wildlife Ventures, Proprietor, Morecambe Bay Centre, 34 Thornton Road, Morecambe, Lancashire, Tel Morecambe 418577 has 7 day bird-watching holidays from April to October. It also offers 7 day combined bird-watching, deer-watching and fell-walking holidays. Age: 15+ (11 if accompanied).

Preston Montford Field Centre, Montford Bridge, Shrewsbury, Shropshire, Tel Montford Bridge 380, has a variety of courses in bird-watching and other natural history topics. Age: 12+.

Reivers of Tarset Ltd, The Comb, Tarset, North Tyne Valley, Northumberland, Tel Greenhaugh 40245 has 7 day multi-activity holidays including wildlife observation. Age: 14+.

Slapton Ley Field Centre, Slapton, Kingsbridge, Devon, Tel Torcross 466 has bird-watching courses. Age: 10+.

Tallard Bay Hotel, Tallard-by-Looe, Cornwall Tel Polperro 228, has 4 night bird-watching holidays. Age: 12+.

Thatched House Hotel, Director, Warner Road, off Clayton Road, Selsey, Chichester, West Sussex, Tel Selsey 2207 has weekend bird-watching holidays. Age: 12+.

Yorkshire Dales National Park, Whernside Cave and Fell Centre, Dent, Sedburgh, Cumbria, Tel Dent 213 has 2-7 day multi-activity holidays including natural history. Age: 14+ (12 if accompanied).

Youth Hostels Association, Trevelyan House, 8 St Stephens Hill, St Albans, Hertfordshire, Tel St Albans 55215, has a 9-day wildlife safari holiday in East Anglia for 13-16 years, and 4-7 day bird-watching holidays organized in conjunction with the RSPB in any one of 20 centres. Age: 11-16.

Information Centres

Although we have listed many centres below, you will find others mentioned throughout the text. Not all are open throughout the year, so try to check before setting out.

Achray: Queen Elizabeth Forest Park Information Centre at David Marshall Lodge off the A821 Aberfoyle-Trossachs Road, one mile north of Aberfoyle, has leaflets about the walks which range from three to fifteen miles, and about the seven mile Achray Forest Drive which offers marvellous views of mountains, lochs and forest.
Arran: Arran Nature Centre at Cladach, Brodick is staffed by really helpful people who will help you with information about wildlife, identify specimens, and will set you off on nature and geology trails.
Aultroy Cottage: Beinn Eighe Nature Conservancy Interpretive Visitors Centre on the A832 north west of Kinlochewe will

help you to appreciate the national nature reserve where you might see pine marten, wild cat, golden eagles and other birds, besides enjoying a walk in this glorious spot which is full of Alpine plants.

Balmacara: Balmacara Visitor Centre is set in marvellous mountain scenery. There is a ranger naturalist service, and guided and self-guided walks.

Bellarena: Magilligan Field Centre has a super small museum which will really open your eyes to the wide variety of birds and plants in the area and will help you to understand the geology too. Muff Glen, which is nearby, and the embankment of Lough Foyle simply swarm with birds.

Bewdley: Wyre Forest Visitor Centre, about three miles from Bewdley on the A456 to Ludlow, is a modern centre with a wildlife exhibition. The audio-visual presentation explains the history of the forest and has information about wildlife habitats. You'll get some idea of forest crafts as well.

Burscough: *see* Birds in the Wild

Buxton: Poole's Cavern Country Park covers 120 acres of woodland. There's an Interpretive Centre with an audio-visual unit.

Colchester: *see* Birds in the Wild

Danby: Danby Lodge National Park Centre is an old shooting lodge now used to provide an interpretive exhibition with illustrated talks and films on life in the North Yorkshire Moors.

Delamere: Delamere Forest Information Centre, about half a mile west of Delamere Station on the B5152, has displays on the region.

Elvaston: Elvaston Castle Country Park has a new Countryside Museum Field Studies Centre and an Information Centre. This park covers 200 acres and has a lakeside nature trail and riding facilities. The Museum is concerned with the countryside as represented in the park and the surrounding area. Excellent displays include natural history with dioramas of habitats.

Foyers: Farigaig Visitor Centre is not far from Foyers and about ten miles from Aberdeen. It has a small exhibition of forestry and wildlife housed in a converted stable.

Grizedale: Grizedale Forest Wildlife Centre has displays with photographic dioramas, an information room, and nearby nature walks. The Spruce Knott Observation Tower offers you the chance to spot birds on nearby water, and to look out for forest fauna. Information, booking and charges can be obtained from the Visitors Centre.

Hamsterley: Hamsterley Information Centre is on the A689 towards Bedburn. Here you will see displays on wildlife, forestry, and the history of the forest.

Horndean: Queen Elizabeth Country Park Centre has displays and an audio-visual presentation of life in the park, both past and present. There is plenty to do in these 1400 acres of downland and forest, including nature trails to follow.

Kielder: Kielder Castle Visitors Centre, not far from Saughtree, concentrates on the Upper Tyne Valley, and on forestry. There's a wildlife observation hide just over a mile from the Castle. You'll get information about charges and bookings from the Chief Forester at the Castle.

Kinross: *see* Birds in the Wild

Lamberhurst: Bewl Bridge Visitors Centre has information about nature conservation at this newly-opened reservoir.

Lawers: Mountain Visitors Centre is about 400 ft up, but you'll be impressed when you get there. You'll see many species of birds, and a surprising number of Alpine flowers. In the Centre there's an exhibition, and it is the start of guided and self-guided trails.

Livady: Roe Valley Country Park has a modern Visitors Centre where there are film shows and natural history talks.

Llanrwst: Forest Information Centre at Gwydyr Uchaf on the B5106 gives a comprehensive picture of life in the forest — habitats, industry, land use, and so on. There are twelve forest trails in the vicinity, one starting from the Centre. Organized tours of the forest can be arranged with prior notification.

Ludlow: Mortimer Forest Museum and Information Centre at Whitecliffe Wood beside the Ludlow-Wigmore road illustrates the history, wildlife and use of the forest today. This Centre is mainly used for educational purposes.

Lyndhurst: New Forest Information Centre is in the public car park on the A35 Southampton-Bournemouth road. It has leaflets about walks and trails and wildlife in the forest.

Malham: Yorkshire Dales National Park Centre has displays, maps and other material for you to browse over, all related to local life.

Merthyr Tydfil: Garwnant Forest Centre is concerned with the forests in the Brecon Beacons. There are exhibitions and walks.

New Galloway: *see* Deer, Clatteringshaws Loch
Peterborough: Ferry Meadows has an excellent Information Centre with regularly changing displays illustrating the wide variety of animals, birds and plants found in the park.
Ponterwyd: Bwich Nant-Yr-Arian Vistors Centre is an interpretation centre with information about habitats, industry and the landscape. It's a good centre for forest walks.
Rhandirmwyn: *see* Birds in the Wild
Rugeley: Belvedere Wildlife Observation Tower, off the Rugeley-Penkridge road, offers an excellent opportunity to study wildlife, particularly the herds of fallow deer. For information on bookings and charges apply to the Chief Forester, Cannock Forest, Rugeley, West Midlands. You can also go on forest trails, but there is no guide. You have to use your eyes and follow coloured markers.
Santon Downham: There's a forest walk here with deer and squirrels to be observed. The trail is marked. The cheap guide is available from the Forestry Commission, Santon Downham, Brandon, Suffolk.
Sedburgh: National Park Centre has a permanent display interpreting the life of the region.
Skegness: Gibraltar Point Visitors Centre has an exhibition which will help you to understand the wildlife and natural features of this 1500 acre coastal reserve.
Thurstaston: Wirral Country Park Visitors Centre has information about nature trails, and guided walks during the summer.
Torridon: Trust Visitors Centre has audio-visual presentations on wildlife. At Mains, not far away, there is a static display on the life of the red deer.
Witley: Witley Common Information Centre has an exhibition on wildlife and an audio-visual programme.

Museums

Seeing stuffed animals and birds in museums is no substitute for the real thing, and in fact some wildlife lovers may prefer not to see them that way. However, it can be useful to find out exactly what a bird or butterfly looks like before trying to spot it in the wild, and sadly, it's probably the only way you'll see some of them.

Places to Visit

Anstruther: *see* Aquaria

Astmoor: Norton Priory has a summer-house with wildlife displays, and offers conducted walks on Mondays. There's a great deal to look at and to do.

Banff: Banff Museum has an exhibition of British birds.

Birchington: Powell-Cotton Museum has a large collection of zoological specimens together with African and Indian jungle scenes and examples of native arts and crafts.

Birmingham: Birmingham City Museum and Art Gallery has the Beale, Chase and Lysaght collection of British birds, and the Bagnall and Whitwell Herbaria. *See* Butterflies, Bees, Insects and Moths.

Bournemouth: Russell-Cotes Art Gallery and Museum has a New Forest diorama with a tape-recorded commentary and worksheets, and an aquarium of freshwater fish.

Brighton: Booth Museum of Natural History has many exhibits, including a magnificent display of birds mounted in their natural habitat.

Burton-on-Trent: Burton-on-Trent Museum and Art Gallery has a new gallery of British birds.

Cambridge: University Museum of Zoology has a good collection of zoological specimens used for teaching and research.

Cardiff: National Museum of Wales has the new impressive Glanely Gallery. You'll walk into the sight and sounds of different kinds of landscape – mountains, lakes, seashore and woods. There are various panoramas with carefully selected and appropriate animals, birds, rocks, and plants. The sound of birdsong is heard, and you'll feel you're actually out in the countryside and not in a museum at all.

Chingford: Epping Forest Museum is concerned with the animals, birds and plants in Epping forest and man's association with the forest.

Colchester: Colchester Museum is concerned primarily with the natural history of Essex.

Dewsbury: Dewsbury Museum and Art Gallery has a good general collection of British natural history exhibits.

Dorchester: Dorchester County Museum doesn't have a large collection on display, but the exhibits related to local natural history are most imaginatively displayed. Its scope covers birds, mammals, reptiles, insects and marine life, and its aim is to make people realize how much must be done to preserve the countryside. There's a remarkable collection of fossils too.
Downe: Downe House, the home of the great naturalist Charles Darwin, looks as if he's just popped out for a moment. You can see see relics of his personal life and his work, the garden and the famous sand-walk.
Eastbourne: *see* Butterflies, Bees, Insects and Moths
Edinburgh: Royal Scottish Museum has a really comprehensive and well-displayed collection of natural history exhibits – birds, animals, insects and butterflies are all there.
Glasgow: Glasgow Art Gallery and Museum offers a really absorbing introduction to the wildlife of Scotland. There's a tremendous amount to see including a British bird gallery, and a series of large groups concerned with the Polar regions, India, Africa and Australia.
Gloucester: Gloucester City Museum and Art Gallery has a fine natural history collection. There's a unique exhibit – it's the horn of the cow from which Dr Edward Jenner obtained the first vaccine.
Haslemere: Halsemere Educational Museum has an excellent collection of British birds and zoological exhibits.
Ilfracombe: Ilfracombe Museum has a good collection of North Devon birds, butterflies, insects and reptiles.
Kendal: Kendal Borough Museum has a display of mammals and birds that's worth wandering around.
Laxfield: *see* Butterflies, Bees, Insects and Moths
Leeds: Leeds City Museum has exhibits illustrating nearly every aspect of natural history relating to Yorkshire.
Liverpool: Merseyside County Museum has natural history displays which include the gallery of World Natural History, and a series of world habitats reconstructed with specimens and sound effects. You'll enjoy a visit here.
Llanrwst: North Wales Museum of Wildlife displays the British Empire Trophy Collection, an impressive display of big game trophies collected around about the turn of the century. Other exhibits depict the wildlife of Snowdonia, and there's a collection of rare birds which comes from all over the world.

You can also have the unusual and interesting experience of seeing how exhibits are prepared for display.
London: Horniman Museum has an extensive collection of animals, birds and insects. *See* Aquaria, London
London: Natural History Museum is absolutely crammed with exhibits. It holds the national collection of animals and plants, both those in existence and those now extinct. You can follow the story of evolution through special displays, go on a number of trails around the museum including one on wildlife in danger, or simply gaze in astonishment at the dinosaurs. There is a Saturday morning club for those who are interested in natural history.
Louth: *see* Butterflies, Bees, Insects and Moths
Manchester: *see* Aquaria
Millport: *see* Aquaria
Newcastle upon Tyne: Hancock Museum has an excellent section devoted to natural history with a particularly good collection of British birds.
New Galloway: *see* Deer, Clatteringshaws Loch
Nottingham: *see* Butterflies, Bees, Insects and Moths
Penrhyn: *see* Butterflies, Bees, Insects and Moths
Portsmouth: *see* Aquaria
Redcar: *see* Aquaria
Rothesay: Buteshire Natural History Society Museum has natural history collections concerned particularly with the region.
Salcombe: *see* Butterflies, Bees, Insects and Moths
Selborne: Gilbert White Museum has relics of this pioneer naturalist who wrote the *Natural History of Selborne.* The Captain Oates Memorial Library has exhibits about Captain Oates, the Antarctic explorer and Frank Oates who explored Africa.
Lewisburn: Border Forest Museum illustrates the history and natural history of the Border Forest.
Spalding: Ayscoughfee Hall and Gardens has the Ashley Maples collection of British birds.
Stromness: Orkney Natural History Museum has collections of zoology, botany, geology and Orkney bygones.
Tring: Tring Zoological Museum has a really enormous collection. The exhibits include mammals, fish, insects, birds and domestic dogs.

Nature Trails

There are thousands of nature trails all over the country – in forests, nature reserves, national parks, the gardens of stately homes, and perhaps even in your local park. We have mentioned them particularly under Information Centres, but they crop up throughout the book. They are a marvellous way of finding out about the natural history of an area, especially if you have an explanatory leaflet to guide you. Most of these leaflets are free, but there's often a small charge for a rather more detailed guide. Usually, but not always, nature trails are free, so if you are thinking of going on one, take a small amount of money with you.

Your local Parks Department will be able to give you information about trails in the area where you live, and perhaps local libraries will have leaflets. Alternatively get in touch with one of the organizations listed below.

Farm trails are a fairly new idea – you are shown all around a farm and learn about the different aspects of animal breeding and cultivation.

Organizations
Nature Trails
Countryside Commission, John Dower House, Crescent Place, Cheltenham, Gloucestershire, has leaflets about nature trails in National and Country Parks.
English Tourist Board, 4 Grosvenor Gardens, London SW1 publishes *Trails in England.* This includes nature trails, farm trails and forest walks.
Forestry Commission, 25 Savile Row, London W1, Tel 01 734 4251 publishes a free booklet *See Your Forests* which has information about nature trails.
Heart of England Tourist Board, PO Box 15, Worcester, publishes an excellent and very cheap booklet *Nature Trails and Wildlife Centres in the Heart of England,* covering Gloucestershire, Hereford and Worcester, Shropshire, Staffordshire, Warwickshire and the West Midlands.
Nature Conservancy Council, 19 Belgrave Square, London SW1, Tel 01 235 3241, and 12 Hope Terrace, Edinburgh, publishes

leaflets about nature trails in National Nature Reserves in England, Scotland and Wales.
Scottish Tourist Board, 23 Ravelston Terrace, Edinburgh publishes *Walks and Trails in Scotland.*
Wales Tourist Board, 3 Castle Street, Cardiff, Tel Cardiff 27281 publishes *Wales Walking.*

Farm Trails

Association of Agriculture, Victoria Chambers, 16/20 Strutton Ground, London W1, produces a free monthly bulletin which lists open days on farms from April-October.
Countryside Commission (see above) has set up some farm trails. Details are in a leaflet, *Farm Trails.*
Greater London Council, Information Officer, County Hall, London SE1 has details of farm trails operating all year round.

Index

Sunday 14.00-18.00.
p 62

Banff Museum. High Street, Bannff, Grampian. Tel Peterhead 2554.
Open: June-September, Tuesday, Thursday, Wednesday 14.00-17.00, Friday, weekends 14.00-17.00.
p 65

Banham Zoo and Woolly Monkey Sanctuary, The Grove, Banham, Norfolk. Tel Quidenham 476.
Open: Daily 10.30-18.30 or dusk if earlier.
p 36

Baronscourt Forest, Newtownstewart Co Tyrone.
Tel Newtownstewart 458.
Open: Throughout the year by appointment only.
pp 17, 26

Bass Rock, North Berwick, Lothian.
p 11

Battersea Park Zoo, Battersea Park, London SW11.
Tel 01 228 9957.
Open: Easter-September, weekdays 13.30-17.30, Saturday, Sunday, Public Holidays 11.00-18.00.
p 40

Beachy Head Nature Trail, Eastborne, Sussex.
Open: Throughout the year.
p 22

Belfast Zoological Gardens, Antrim Road, Newtownabbey.
Tel Belfast 776277.
Open: Daily March-October 9.00-18.00; November-February 10.30-15.30.
p 37

Belton House Park and Gardens, Belton, Grantham, Lincolnshire. Tel Grantham 66116.
Open: Easter-September Monday-Friday 12.00-17.30, Sunday 14.00-18.00.
p 24

Belvedere Wildlife Observation Tower, Rugeley, West Midlands.
p 64

Beinn Eighe Nature Conservancy Interpretive Visitors Centre, Aultroy Cottage, Kinlochewe.
p 61

Bentley Wildfowl Collection, Halland, Lewes, E Sussex.
Tel Halland 260.
Open: Easter-September daily 11.00-18.00.
p 6

Berkeley Castle, Berkeley, Gloucestershire.
Tel Berkeley 332.
Open: April, September Tuesday-Saturday 14.00-17.00; May-August, Tuesday-Saturday 11.00-17.00, Sunday 14.00-17.00; October Sunday 14.00-16.30; Bank Holiday Mondays 11.00-17.00.
p 25

Bewl Bridge Visitors Centre, Bewl Bridge Reservoir, Lamberhurst, Sussex.
p 63

Bickleigh Mill Farm, Bickleigh, Nr Tiverton, Devon.
Tel Bickleigh 419. Get in touch for opening times.
p 44

Birdland, Bourton-on-the-Water, Gloucestershire.
Tel Bourton-on-the-Water 20689.
Open: Daily March-November 10.00-18.00; December-February 10.30-16.00.
pp 2, 5

Bird Paradise, Hayle, Cornwall.
Tel Hayle 753365.
Open: Daily 10.00-dusk.
p 7

Birdworld Zoological Gardens, Holt Pound, Farnham, Surrey.
Tel Bentley (Hants) 2140.
Open: Daily 9.30-18.00 (or one hour before dusk).
p 6

Birmingham City Museum and Art Gallery, Chamberlain Square, Birmingham, W Midlands.
Tel 021 235 2834.
Open: Monday-Saturday 10.00-17.30.
pp 22, 65

Blackpool Tower Buildings and Circus, The Promenade, Blackpool, Lancashire.
Tel Blackpool 25252.
Open: May-October daily 9.30-23.00.
pp 2, 5, 22

Blackpool Zoo Park, East Park Drive, Blackpool, Lancashire.
Tel Blackpool 65027.
Open: Daily 10.00-18.00 or dusk,
p 37

Blacktoft Sands, S Humberside.
p 12

Blakeney Point Nature Reserve, Point House, Norston, Norfolk.
Tel Clay 220.
p 12

Bleans Woods, Canterbury, Kent.
p 13

Bodmin Farm Park, Fletchers Bridge, Bodmin, Cornwall.
Open: Spring Bank Holiday, Whitsun-end September, Sunday-Friday 10.00-18.00 (weather permitting).
p 44

Bolton Aquarium, Civic Centre, Bolton, Greater Manchester.
p 2

Booth Museum of Natural History, Dyke Road, Brighton, Sussex.
Tel Brighton 552586.
Open: Monday, Tuesday, Wednesday, Friday, Saturday 10.00-17.00, Sunday 14.00-17.00.
p 65

Border Forest Museum, Lewisburn, Northumberland.
Open: Easter-late July, Saturday, Sunday 14.00-17.00; Late July-August, daily 14.00-17.00; September, Saturday and Sunday 14.00-17.00.
p 67

Bourstall Duck Decoy and Nature Reserve, Brill, Buckinghamshire.
Tel Brill 488.
Open: February-early September Tuesday-Sunday, Bank Holiday Mondays 10.00-17.00.
p 12

Brancaster Staithe National Nature Reserve, Norfolk.
p 12

Brean Down Bird Garden, Brean, Somerset. Tel Brean Down 209.
Open: March-October daily 10.00-19.30 (last entry two hours before dusk).
p 5

Brighton Aquarium and Dolphinarium, Marine Parade, Brighton, Sussex.
Tel Brighton 64233.
Open: Daily 9.00-18.30.
p 2

Bristol Zoological Gardens, Clifton Down, Bristol, Avon.
Tel Bristol 38951.
Open: Weekdays from 9.00, Sunday from 10.00 (closing time varies).
p 37

British Beekeepers Association, c/o National Agricultural Centre, Stoneleigh, Kenilworth, Warwickshire. Tel Kenilworth 56151.
p 23

Brixham Aquarium, Brixham, Devon.
Open: Daily in Summer months from 10.00.
p 2

Broadland Conservation Centre, Ranworth Inner Broad, Norfolk.
Tel South Walsham 479.
Open: Tuesday-Sunday 10.00-17.00, Saturday 14.00-17.00.
p 18

Brook, Isle of Wight.
p 12

Brownsea Island, Poole Harbour, Dorset.
Open: April-September daily 10.00-19.00 or dusk.
p 17

Broxbourne Zoo, White Stubbs Lane, Broxbourne, Hertfordshire.
Tel Hoddesdon 62852.
Open: Daily 10.00-18.00 (until 17.00 in winter).
p 37

Burton Mere, Burton Bradstock, Dorset.
p 13

Burton-on-Trent Museum and Art Gallery, Guild Street, Burton-on-Trent, Staffordshire.
Tel Burton-on-Trent 63042.
Open: Monday-Friday 11.00-18.00, Saturday 11.00-17.00.
p 65

Bushy Park, Teddington, Middlesex.
Open: Daily.
p 25

Buteshire Natural History Society Museum, Stuart Street, Rothesay, Bute, Strathclyde.
Open: April-October weekdays 10.30-12.30, 14.30-16.30; June-September also Sunday 14.30-16.30; November-March Tuesday-Saturday 14.30-16.30.
p 67

Bwich Nant-Yr-Arian Forest Visitor Centre, Ponterwyd, Dyfed.
Open: Easter-October 10.00-17.00; July, August until 19.00.
p 64

Caerlaverock Branch of the Wildfowl Trust, Caerlaverock, Dumfries and Galloway.
Tel Glencaple 200.
Open: September-mid May (guided tours at 11.00, 14.00).
p 13

Calderpark Zoo, Uddingston, Glasgow. Tel 041 771 1185.
Open: Daily 9.30-19.00 (or 17.00 depending on the season).
p 39

Calf of Man, Isle of Man.
p 13

Cameron Loch Lomond, Balloch, Strathclyde.
Tel Alexandria 57211.
Open: April-September daily 10.00-18.00.
p 33

Cannock Forest Information Centre, nr Rugeley, Staffordshire. Tel Rugeley 2035.
p 64

Cannon Hill Nature Centre, Cannon Hill Park, Birmingham, West Midlands. Tel 021 472 7775.
Open: Easter-August, Bank Holidays 10.00-18.00; September-Easter, weekdays 10.00-16.00, Sunday 13.00-16.00, closed Tuesday.
pp 12, 44

Castle Ward, Strangford, Co Down.
Tel Strangford 204.
Open: Daily during daylight hours.
p 8

Causeway Safari Park, Benwarden, Dervock, Co Antrim.
Tel Dervock 476.
Open: Easter; May-mid September daily 10.00-18.30.
p 38

Chessington Zoo, Chessington, Surrey. Tel Epsom 27227.
Open: Daily April-September 9.30-17.00; October-March 10.00-16.00.
p 37

Chester Zoo and Gardens, Chester, Cheshire. Tel Chester 20106.
Open: Daily 9.00-dusk.
pp 28, 37

Child-Beale Wildfowl Trust, Church Farm, Basildon-on-Thames, Berkshire. Tel Upper Basildon 325.
Open: Good Friday-September, Wednesday, Thursday, Saturday, Sunday, Bank Holidays 11.30-18.30.
p 36

Chilham Castle, Chilham, Kent.
Tel Chilham 319.
Open: Gardens Easter-October,

Tuesday-Thursday, Saturday, Sunday (afternoons only).

p 28

Chillingham Park, Chillingham, Northumberland.
Tel Chatton 213.
Open: April-October, weekdays (not Tuesday), Bank Holidays 10.00-12.00, 14.00-17.00, Sunday 14.00-17.00 (tickets from the keeper's cottage).

p 44

Claw Moor, Information from Forestry Commission, Cookworthy Moor, Beaworthy, Devon.

p 13

Clee Hill Bird and Animal Gardens, Cleobury Mortimer, Salop.
Tel Clee Hillstone 274.
Open: Daily Summer 10.00-18.00; Winter 10.00-16.00.

p 38

Cley Marshes Nature Reserve, Chief Warden, Watcher's Cottage, Cley-next-the-Sea, Norfolk.
Tel Cley 380 for information and bookings; admission by permit issued in advance.

p 14

Clumber Park, Worksop, Nottinghamshire.

p 20

Cockle Island, Ballymacormick Point, Co Down.
Open: See text.

p 11

Coed Alt Butterfly Reserve, Ystwyth Forest, nr Aberystwyth, Dyfed (approach via Black Covert Forest Walk).

p 23

Colchester Museum of Natural History, All Saints' Church, High Street, Colchester, Essex.
Tel Colchester 73669
Open: April-September weekdays 10.00-13.00, 14.00-17.00 (October-March Saturday closing at 16.00).

p 65

Colchester Zoo, Stanway Hall, Colchester, Essex.
Tel Colchester 330253.
Open: Daily 9.30-19.30 or one hour before sunset.

p 38

Coombe Abbey Bird Garden, Coombe Countryside Park, Brinklow Road, Coventry, W Midlands.
Tel Coventry 453500.
Open: Daily 10.00-dusk.

p 6

Coombe Wood, Croydon, Surrey.

p 14

Copeland Islands, reached from Donaghadee, Co Down.

p 14

Coton Wildfowl Gardens, Coton, Northamptonshire.
Tel Northampton 740219.
Open: Easter-October, Sunday, Thursday, Bank Holidays 14.00-18.00; July and August also Wednesday.

p 6

Cotswold Farm Park, Guiting Power, Cheltenham, Gloucestershire.
Tel Guiting Power 307.
Open: May-October 10.30-18.00.

p 45

Courage Shire Horse Centre, Cherry Garden Lane, Bath Road, Maidenhead Thicket, Maidenhead, Berkshire.
Tel Littlewick Green 3917.
Open: March-October Tuesday-Sunday, Bank Holiday Mondays 11.00-17.00.

p 46

Coventry Zoo Park, Whitley Common, Coventry, W Midlands.
Tel Coventry 301772.

Open: Daily 10.00-dusk.
p 38
Cricket St Thomas Wild Life Park, Chard, Somerset. Tel Winsham 396.
Open: Daily 10.00-18.00.
p 38
Cromer Zoo, Howard's Hill, Cromer, Norfolk.
Tel Cromer 2947.
Open: Daily 10.00-19.00 or dusk.
p 38
Crystal Palace Zoo, Thicket Road, London SE19.
Tel 01 778 4487.
Open: Easter School Holidays-September, Monday-Friday 13.00-18.00, Saturday, Sunday Bank Holidays, School Holidays 11.00-18.00.
p 40
Cumberland House Museum and Aquarium, Eastern Parade, Southsea, Hampshire.
Tel Portsmouth 32654.
Open: Daily 10.30-17.30.
pp 3, 67
Curraghs Wild Life Park, Ballaugh, Isle of Man.
Tel Sulby 323.
Open: Easter, May-September daily 10.00-18.00.
p 36

Dalkeith Park, Dalkeith, Lothian, or Buccleight Enterprises Ltd.
Tel Selkirk 20732.
p 44
Danby Lodge National Park Centre, Danby, N Yorkshire.
Open: Easter-October daily 10.00-18.00; November, March, Saturday, Sunday 10.00-17.00.
p 62
Danes Dyke Nature Trail, Bridlington, Humberside.
p 12
Dartmoor Wildlife Park, Sparkwell, Devon.
Tel Cornwood 209.
Open: Daily 10.00-dusk.
p 46
Delamere Bird Gardens, Fladbury, Hereford and Worcester.
Tel Evesham 860580.
Open: Daily 9.30-dusk.
pp 2, 6, 22
Delamere Forest Information Centre, Cheshire.
Open: Monday-Friday 7.30-16.00.
p 62
Dewsbury Museum and Art Gallery, Crow Nest Park, Dewsbury, Yorkshire.
Tel Dewsbury 468171.
Open: April-September, Tuesday-Sunday (not Friday) 13.30-19.30; October-March, Tuesday-Thursday, Saturday 13.30-16.30.
p 65
Dinas Nature Trail, Rhandirmwyn, Dyfed.
Open: Throughout the year.
pp 18, 64
Dorchester County Museum, High West Street, Dorchester, Dorset.
Tel Dorchester 2735.
Open: Monday-Friday 10.00-17.00.
p 66
Downe House, Downe, Kent.
Open: Tuesday, Wednesday, Thursday, Saturday, Sunday, Bank Holiday Mondays 13.00-18.00.
p 66
Drayton Manor Park and Zoo, Fazely, Staffordshire.
Tel Tamworth 68481.
Open: Easter-October daily 10.30-19.00.
p 39
Dreamland Park Zoo, Dreamland Amusement Park, Margate, Kent.

Tel Thanet 21212.
Open: Mid May-September daily.
p 41

Drum Manor, Gortin Glen, Cookstown, Co Tyrone.
Tel Cookstown 2774.
Open: Daily 10.00-dusk.
pp 6, 14, 22

Drusillas Zoo Park, Alfriston, E Sussex. Tel Alfriston 870234.
Open: April-October daily 11.00-18.00; November-March Saurday and Sunday 11.00-dusk.
p 36

Dudley Zoo, 2 The Broadway, Dudley, W Midlands.
Tel Dudley 52401.
Open: Daily 10.00-dusk.
p 39

Dunvegan Castle, Dunvegan, Isle of Skye.
Open: Easter-mid October 14.00-17.00; mid June-mid September from 10.30.
p 31

Dyrham Park, Chippenham, Avon.
Open: Easter-September daily 14.00-18.00, Bank Holidays 12.00-18.00; October, November, March weekends only.
p 25

Easton Farm Park, Wickham Market, Suffolk.
Open: End March-September, Tuesday-Sunday 10.30-18.00.
pp 23, 47

Ebbor Gorge National Nature Reserve, Wookey Hole, Wells, Somerset.
p 23

Edgbaston Botanical Gardens, Edgbaston, Warwickshire.
Open: Daily.
pp 5, 45

Edinburgh Zoo, Zoological Park, Murrayfield, Edinburgh.
Tel 031 334 9171.
Open: Daily 9.00-21.00 (until 17.00 or dusk in winter).
pp 28, 39

Elsham Hall Country Park, Elsham, Humberside.
Tel Barnetby 738.
Open: Monday-Friday 12.00-20.00 or dusk, Saturday, Sunday Bank Holidays 11.00-20.00 or dusk; November-March, Monday-Friday 14.00-16.30, Saturday, Sunday 11.00-16.30.
p 44

Elvaston Castle Country Park, Elvaston, Derby.
Tel Derby 71342.
Open: Daily until dusk.
Museum
Open: April-October daily 12.00-16.00 (Summer weekends until 18.00).
p 62

Emberton Park Nature Trail, Olney, Northamptonshire.
p 22

Epping Forest Museum, Queen Elizabeth's Hunting Lodge, Chingford, London E4.
Open: Wednesday-Sunday 14.00-18.00.
p 65

Exmouth Aquarium, Exmouth, Devon.
Open: Easter-September, daily; October-Easter, Tuesday, Friday and Saturday.
p 2

Fairhaven Garden Trust, South Walsham, Norfolk.
Tel South Walsham 449.
Open: Easter Saturday and Monday, early April-late September, Thursday, Saturday, Sunday 14.00-18.00.
p 18

Fair Isle Bird Observatory, Fair Isle.

Open: November-March.
p 14
Falconry Centre, Newent, Gloucestershire.
Tel Newent 820286.
Open: Wednesday-Monday 10.30-17.30 or dusk.
p 28
Farigaig Visitors' Centre, Foyers, Highland.
p 62
Farne Islands, nr Bamburgh, Northumberland.
Open: Inner Farne and Staple Islands, April-September (restricted access in breeding season, May-July). For permission to land at other times apply to Warden/Naturalist, The Sheiling, 8 St Aiden's, Seahouses, Northumberland.
Tel Seahouses 720651.
pp 14, 31
Farway Country Park, Farway, Colyton, Devon.
Tel Farway 224.
Open: Good Friday-September, Sunday-Friday, Bank Holiday Saturday 10.00-18.00 (last entry 17.00).
p 44
Ferry Meadows, Ham Lane, Orton Waterville, Peterborough, Cambridgeshire.
Tel Peterborough 234443.
p 64
Fetlar Island, Shetlands.
Open: (see text).
p 14
Fingrinhoe Nature Reserve, Colchester, Essex.
p 14
Flamborough Head, Yorkshire.
p 15
Flamingo Gardens and Zoological Park, Weston Underwood, Buckinghamshire. Tel Bedford 711451.
Open: Good Friday-September Wednesday, Thursday, Saturday, Sunday, Bank Holidays 14.00-20.00.
p 8
Flamingo Park Bird Sanctuary, Seaview, Isle of Wight.
Tel Seaview 2153.
Open: April or Easter-May, Saturday and Sunday 14.00-18.00; June-September, Monday-Saturday 10.30-18.00, Sunday 14.00-18.00.
p 8
Forest Information Centre, Llanrwst, Gwynedd.
Tel Llanwrst 640578.
Open: Easter-October daily 10.00-17.00.
p 63
Forestry Commission, 231 Corstorphine Road, Edinburgh; 25 Saville Row, London W1.
p 57
Furze Farm Park, Bridgerule, Nr Holsworthy, W Devon.
Tel Bridgerule 342.
Open: Daily 10.00-dusk (check times of opening and closing).
p 44

Galloway Deer Museum, Clatteringshaws Loch, Dumfries and Galloway.
Open: April-September.
pp 25, 64, 67
Garwnant Forest Centre, nr Merthyr Tydfil, Mid Glamorgan.
Tel Merthyr Tydfil 3060.
Open: Easter-September weekdays 9.00-16.00; July, August also Wednesday and Thursday 6.00-20.00, Saturday and Sunday 13.00-18.00; April, September Saturday and Sunday 14.00-16.00; May, Saturday and Sunday 14.00-17.00; June, Saturday and Sunday 14.00-18.00;

Bank Holidays 12.00-18.00.
p 63
Gibraltar Point Visitor Centre, nr Skegness, Lincolnshire. Open: mid May-September, Monday-Friday, Sunday 10.00-13.00, 14.00-17.00, Saturday 14.00-17.00; also early June-August evenings 18.00-21.00.
pp 18, 64
Gilbert White Museum, The Wakes, Selborne, Hampshire. Tel Selborne 275. Open: March-October Tuesday-Sunday 12.00-17.30.
p 67
Glanton World Bird Research Station, Glanton, Northumberland. Tel Powburn 257. Open: June-September daily 14.00-18.00.
p 15
Glasgow Art Gallery and Museum, Kelvingrove Park, Glasgow. Tel 041 334 1134. Open: Weekdays 10.00-17.00, Sunday 14.00-17.00.
p 66
Glendaruel Forest, Forestry Office at Tighnabruaich, Strathclyde.
p 15
Glenmore Forest Park, Loch Morlich, nr Aviemore, Highland.
p 25
Gloucester City Museum and Art Gallery, Brunswick Road, Gloucester. Tel Gloucester 24131. Open: Weekdays 10.00-17.00.
p 66
Goatfell, Brodick, Arran.
p 12
Gosford Forest Park, Markethill, Co Armagh. Tel Markethill 277. Open: Throughout the year.
p 17
Grafham Water, Buckden, Norfolk.
p 13
Great Orme's Head, Llandudno, Gwynedd.
p 16
Grizedale Forest Wildlife Centre, Grizedale, Cumbria. Tel Satterthwaite 273. Open: Daily, Easter-October 10.00-17.00; October-Easter 11.00-16.00.
p 62
Guilsborough Grange Bird and Pet Park, West Haddon Road, Northamptonshire. Tel Guilsborough 278. Open: early March-October daily 11.00-19.00.
p 6
Gull Rocks, Holywell, Cornwall.
p 16
Gwenffrwd and Dinas Forest, Dyfed, Wales. Open: Nature trail at Dinas daily throughout the year; at Gwenffrwd mid April-August Monday, Wednesday, Saturday.
p 15
Gwydyr Visitor Centre, Gwydyr Forest, Llanrwst, Gwynedd. Open: Easter-October daily 10.00-17.00.
p 15

Hamsterley Information Centre, nr Barnard Castle, Willington, Bishop Auckland, Durham.
p 63
Hancock Museum, Barras Bridge, University of Newcastle-upon-Tyne. Tel Newcastle-upon-Tyne 22359. Open: Weekdays 10.00-17.00; Easter-September also Sunday 14.00-17.00.
p 67
Handa Island Bird Sanctuary,

off Isle of Scourie.
p 15
Harewood House and Bird Garden, Harewood, nr Leeds, W Yorkshire. Tel Harewood 886225.
Open: Good Friday-October daily from 11.00; November, March Wednesday and Sunday from 11.00.
pp 6, 22
Haslemere Educational Museum, High Street, Haslemere, Surrey. Tel Haslemere 2112.
Open: April-October, Tuesday-Saturday 10.00-17.00, Sunday 14.00-17.00; November-March Tuesday-Saturday 10.00-16.00.
p 66
Haugh Wood, Woolhope Hall, Hereford and Worcester.
p 20
Havergate Island, Orford, Suffolk.
p 17
Heathfield Wildlife Park, Heathfield, E Sussex. Tel Heathfield 4748.
Open: Daily 10.00-18.00 or dusk.
p 40
Henley Bird Gardens, High Street, Henley-in-Arden, Warwickshire. Tel Henley-in-Arden 2562.
Open: Early April-October Sunday 10.30-18.00.
p 7
Hickling Broad Water Trail and Nature Reserve, Hickling, Norfolk. Tel Hickling 276. For advance reservations telephone between 8.00 and 9.00, or 12.45-13.15.
Open: End May-mid September. Admission by permit only issued in advance for reserve.
p 15
Highland Wildlife Park, Kincraig, Aviemore, Highland. Tel Doune 456.
Open: Mid March-October daily from 10.00.
pp 32, 45
Hilbre Island, Liverpool.
p 16
Hirsel House, Coldstream, Roxburghshire.
p 14
Holker Hall, Cark-in-Cartmel, Grange-over-Sands, Cumbria. Tel Flookburgh 328.
Open: Easter-September daily Sunday-Friday 11.00-18.00.
p 25
Holme Nature Reserve, Warden, The Firs, Holme-next-the-Sea, Hunstanton, Norfolk. Tel Holme 240 for information and bookings. Admission is by permit only issued in advance.
p 16
Hopetoun House, South Queensferry, Lothian.
Open: Early May-mid September Saturday-Wednesday 13.30-17.30.
p 26
Horniman Museum, 100 London Road, Forest Hill, London SE23. Tel 01 699 2339.
Open: Monday-Saturday 10.30-18.00, Sunday 14.00-18.00.
pp 2, 22, 67
Howlett's Zoo Park, Bekesbourne, Kent. Tel Hythe 60618.
Open: Daily 10.00-18.00.
p 37

Ilfracombe Museum, Wilder Road, Ilfracombe, Devon.
Open: Daily from 10.00.
p 66
Inverpolly Information Centre, Knockan Cliff, nr Inverpolly, Highland.
p 16
Isle of Rhum National Conservation Centre, Kinloch Glen, Rhum.
pp 25, 66

Jersey Zoological Park,

Les Augres Manor, Gorey, Jersey. Tel Jersey Central 61949.
Open: Daily May-September 10.00-18.00; October-April 10.00-17.00.
p 39

Kelling Park Aviaries, Weybourne Road, Holt, Norfolk. Tel Holt 2235.
Open: Daily 10.00-dusk.
p 7

Kendal Museum, Station Road, Kendal, Cumbria. Tel Kendal 21374.
Open: Weekdays 10.30-17.00.
p 66

Kielder Castle Forest Centre, Northumberland. Tel Kielder 50259.
Open: Spring Bank Holiday-September, weekdays 8.00-12.00, 13.00-16.00, Weekends, Bank Holidays 12.00-18.00.
pp 16, 63

Kilverstone Wild Life Park, Kilverstone, Norfolk. Tel Thetford 5369.
Open: Daily 10.00-18.30 or dusk.
p 42

Kingsford Bridge Marsh Reserve, Colchester, Essex.
pp 14, 62

Kinnoull Hill, nr Perth, Tayside.
p 26

Knaresborough Zoological Gardens, Conyingham Hall, Knaresborough, N Yorkshire.
Open: Daily 10.00-20.00 (until 16.00 in winter).
p 40

Knebworth House, Knebworth, Hertfordshire. Tel 043 881 2661.
Open: Easter-September Tuesday-Sunday; October Sunday.
p 25

Knole Park, Sevenoaks, Kent.
Open: Park open daily.
p 26

Knowsley Safari Park, Liverpool, Merseyside. Tel 051 430 9009.
Open: Daily 10.00-17.30 (until 16.00 in winter).
pp 3, 33

Lambton Pleasure Park, Lambton, Co Durham. Tel Fencehouses 3311.
Open: March-October daily 10.00-17.00.
p 33

Laxfield District Museum, Guildhall, Laxfield, Suffolk. Tel Ubbeston 369.
Open: Spring Bank Holiday Monday-mid September Saturday and Sunday 14.00-17.30.
pp 22, 66

Leeds City Museum, Municipal Buildings, Leeds. Tel Leeds 31301, ext 532.
Open: Weekdays 10.00-18.30.
p 66

Lilford Park, Lilford, nr Oundle, Peterborough, Northamptonshire. Tel Clopton 648.
Open: Easter-October daily 10.00-20.00 or dusk.
pp 7, 45

Lindos Bird Farm, 72 Green Road, Conlig, Bangor, Gwynedd. Tel Bangor 6983.
Open: Monday-Friday 13.00-dusk, Saturday, Sunday 10.00-dusk.
p 6

Linn Park, Glasgow.
Open: Daily, 7.00-dusk.
p 45

Loch Druidilberg, South Uist, Outer Hebrides.
p 16

Loch Garten Nature Reserve, Highlands, Scotland.
p 16

Loch of Lowes Nature Reserve, Dunkeld, Tayside. Tel Dunkeld 337 (April-September) Ballintuig 267 (October-March).

Open: April, May, September 10.00-19.00; June-August 10.00-20.30.
p 16
London Zoo, Regent's Park, London NW1. Tel 01 722 3333.
Open: March-October weekdays 9.00-18.00 or dusk, Sunday, Bank Holidays 9.00-19.00 or dusk; November-February daily 10.00 to dusk.
pp 28, 40
Longleat House, Longleat, Wiltshire. Tel Maiden Bradley 551.
Open: Daily, Easter-September 10.00-18.00; October-Easter 10.00-16.00.
p 33
Looe Aquarium, The Quay, Looe, Cornwall.
Open: June-September daily 10.00-18.00 (until 21.00 June-mid September).
p 2
Louth Naturalists Antiquarian and Literary Society Museum, 4 Broadbank, Louth.
Tel Louth 3026.
Open: Wednesday 13.45-16.00, Saturday 14.15-16.30, Sunday 14.30-16.30. August also Thursday 14.15-16.30.
pp 22, 67
Lullingstone Silk Farm *see* Worldwide Butterflies Ltd.
p 23
Lunga Wildlife Reserve, Ardfern, Strathclyde. Tel Barbreck 640.
Open: Easter-September daily 11.00-18.00.
p 43
Lyme Park, Disley, nr Stockport, Cheshire.
Park open daily 8.00-dusk.
p 25

Mablethorpe Animal and Bird Gardens, North End, Mablethorpe, Lincolnshire.
Tel Mablethorpe 3346.
Open: Easter-October 10.00-20.00 (or 1 hour before dusk).
pp 22, 45
Magilligan Field Centre, Bellarena, Londonderry.
p 62
Manchester Museum, Oxford Road, Manchester University, Manchester.
Tel 063 273 3333.
Open: Monday-Saturday 10.00-17.00 (Wednesday until 21.00).
pp 2, 67
Manor House Wildlife and Leisure Park, St Florence, nr Tenby, Dyfed.
Tel Carew 201.
Open: Easter-September 10.00-18.00.
pp 8, 26, 46
Marine Biological Association Aquarium, Plymouth, Devon.
Open: Weekdays, Bank Holidays.
p 3
Marine Biological Station Aquarium, Port Erin, Isle of Man.
Open: Weekdays 10.00-17.00.
p 3
Marineland Oceanarium and Aquarium, The Jetty, Morecambe, Lancashire. Tel Morecambe 414727.
Open: Daily, Summer 10.00-19.30; Winter 10.00-16.30.
p 2
Martin Mere Branch of the Wildfowl Trust, Martin Mere, Burscough, Nr Ormskirk, Lancashire.
Tel Burscough 895181.
Open: Daily 9.30-dusk.
pp 13, 62
Marwell Zoological Park, Colden Common, nr Winchester, Hampshire.
Tel Owslebury 206.
Open: Daily 10.00-18.00 or dusk.
p 43
Merley Bird Gardens, Merley, nr Wimbourne, Dorset.
Tel Wimbourne 3790.

Open: Daily 10.30-18.30.
p 8
Merseyside County Museum,
William Brown Street,
Liverpool 3. Tel 051 207 0001.
Open: Weekdays 10.00-17.00,
Sunday 14.00-17.00.
pp 2, 66
Minsmere Bird Sanctuary, Dunwich,
Suffolk.
p 14
Mole Hall Wildlife Park, Newport,
Essex. Tel Saffron Walden 40400.
Open: Daily 10.30-18.00.
p 41
Monkey Sanctuary, Murraytown,
Looe, Cornwall.
Tel Looe 2532.
Open: April-September daily
10.30-17.30.
p 41
Mortimer Forest Museum and Information Centre, Ludlow,
Shropshire.
pp 26, 63
Mountain Visitor Centre, Lawers,
Tayside. Tel Killin 397.
Open: Good Friday-May
Weekdays 11.00-16.00, Sunday
10.00-17.30; June-September daily
10.00-17.30.
p 63
Muncaster Castle, Muncaster,
Cumbria. Tel Ravenglass 614.
Open: Grounds Easter-September
daily (not Friday) 12.00-17.00.
p 7

National Museum of Wales,
Cathays Park, Cardiff, Glamorgan.
Tel Cardiff 397951.
Open: April-September, weekdays
10.00-18.00, Sunday 14.30-17.00;
October-March weekdays
10.00-17.00, Sunday 14.30-17.00.
p 65
National Park Centre, 72 Main
Street, Sedbergh, Cumbria.
Tel Sedbergh 20125.
Open: April-September daily
mid morning-late afternoon.
p 64
Natural History Collection,
Godshill, Isle of Wight.
Open: April-September daily.
p 2
Natural History Museum,
Cromwell Road,
South Kensington, London SW7.
Tel 01 589 6323.
Open: Weekdays 10.00-18.00,
Sunday 14.30-18.00.
p 67
Natureland Marine Zoo,
North Parade, The Promenade,
Skegness, Lincolnshire.
Tel Skegness 4345.
Open: Daily, May-September
10.00-19.30; October-April
10.00-16.00.
p 3
Needles Headland, Alum Bay,
Isle of Wight.
p 17
New Forest Information Centre,
Lyndhurst, Hampshire.
Open: Easter-September daily
9.30-12.30, 13.30-17.00.
pp 26, 63
New Linton Zoological Gardens,
Mortimer House,
Hadstock Road, Linton,
Cambridgeshire.
Tel Cambridge 891308.
Open: Daily 10.00-19.00 or dusk.
p 40
Newham Grange Leisure Farm,
Coulby Newham,
Middlesbrough, Cleveland.
Open: Daily 10.00-18.30.
p 44
Newquay Marine Aquarium,
Newquay, Cornwall.
Open: June-September daily.
p 3
Newquay Zoo, Trenance Leisure
Park, Newquay, Cornwall.
Tel Newquay 3342.

Open: Daily 10.00-dusk.
pp 3, 41
Newtown Marsh, Isle of Wight.
p 17
Norfolk Wildlife Park,
Great Witchingham, Norfolk.
Tel Great Witchingham 274.
Open: Daily 10.30-18.00 or sunset.
pp 28, 45
Northey Island, nr Maldon, Essex.
p 17
North Wales Museum of Wildlife,
Fron Ganol, School Bank Road,
Llanrwst, Gwynedd.
Tel Llanrwst 640664.
Open: Summer, weekdays, Bank Holidays 9.30-18.30, Sunday 10.30-18.30; Winter, Monday-Friday 10.00-16.00.
p 66
Norton Bird Gardens,
Bury St Edmunds, Suffolk.
p 5
Norton Priory, nr Astmoor,
Runcorn, Cheshire.
Tel Runcorn 69895.
Open: Easter-September, Monday-Wednesday 13.00-17.00, Saturday, Sunday, Bank Holidays 13.00-18.00.
p 65
Noss Nature Reserve, Noss Island, Shetlands.
p 17
Nottingham Natural History Museum,
Wollaton Hall, Nottingham.
Tel Nottingham 281333.
Open: April-September weekdays 10.00-19.00, Sunday 14.00-17.00; October-March weekdays 10.00-dusk, Sunday 13.30-16.30.
pp 22, 26, 67

Oceanarium and Aquarium,
Stone Jetty, Marine Road,
Morecambe, Lancashire.
Tel Morecambe 41474.
Open: Mid May-mid October daily 10.00-19.30; mid October-mid May daily 10.00-16.30.
p 2
Olney, Northamptonshire.
p 22
Orkney Natural History Museum,
52 Alfred Street, Stromness,
Orkney. Tel Stromness 246.
Open: Weekdays 11.00-12.30, 13.30-17.00 (Thursday until 13.00); July-August open at 10.00.
p 67
Otter Trust, Earsham, nr Bungay,
Suffolk. Tel Bungay 3470.
Open: March-November daily 10.30-18.00 or sunset. Grounds closed December-February.
pp 30, 31
Overbecks Museum, Sharpitor,
Salcombe, Devon.
Open: April-October daily 11.00-13.00, 14.00-18.00.
pp 23, 67
Oxford Island Nature Reserve,
Warden, Lurgan, Craigauor,
Co Armagh. Tel Lurgan 2205.
Open: Throughout the year.
p 16
Paignton Seashore Aquarium,
The Harbour, Paignton, Devon.
Open: End May-September daily.
pp 3, 41
Paignton Zoo and Botanical Gardens, Totnes Road, Paignton,
Devon. Tel Paignton 557872.
Open: Daily 10.00-19.30 (until 17.30 in Winter).
p 41
Palacerigg Country Park,
Palacerigg, Cumbernauld,
Central, Scotland.
Open: Throughout the year from dawn to dusk.
p 46
Peakirk Branch of the Wildfowl Trust, nr Peterborough,
Cambridgeshire.
Tel Peterborough 252271.

Open: Daily 9.30-16.30.
p 17
Penrhyn Castle, Bangor, Gwynedd, Wales.
Tel Bangor 53084.
Open: June-September, Monday-Friday, Bank Holidays 11.00-17.00; April, May, October daily 14.00-17.00.
pp 23, 67
Penscynor Wildlife Park, Cilfrew, Neath, W Glamorgan. Tel Neath 2189.
Open: Daily 10.00-18.00.
pp 2, 5
Penzance Aquarium, Barbican Crafts Centre, Penzance, Cornwall.
p 3
Plymouth Aquarium *see* Marine Biological Association.
p 3
Poole Park Zoo, Poole, Dorset.
Tel Parkstone 745296.
Open: March-October 10.00-18.00 or dusk; November-February, Saturday, Sunday, Public Holidays, local school holidays 10.00-dusk.
p 42
Poole's Cavern Country Park, Green Lane, Buxton, Derbyshire.
Open: Daily.
p 62
Port Lympne Wildlife Sanctuary, Lympne, Kent. Tel Hythe 60618.
Open: Daily 10.00-18.00 or sunset.
p 41
Powell-Cotton Museum, Quex Park, Birchington, Kent.
Tel Birchington 42168.
Open: Early April-September, Sunday, Wednesday, Thursday; mid July-early September Tuesday-Friday, Sunday; October-March, Thursday (check for exact times).
p 65
Prinknash Bird Park, Cranham, Gloucestershire.
Tel Painswick 812727.
Open: March-October daily 10.00-18.00; November-February, Saturday and Sunday 11.00-16.00 (or one hour before sunset).
p 6

Queen Elizabeth Country Park Centre, Gravel Hill, Horndean, Nr Portsmouth, Hampshire.
Tel Horndean 595040.
Open: April-October 10.00-18.00; November, February, March 10.00-dusk; December and January, Saturday 13.00-dusk, Sunday 10.00-dusk.
p 63
Queen Elizabeth Forest Park Information Centre, David Marshall Lodge, Aberfoyle, Central.
p 61

Raby Castle, Staindrop, Co Durham.
Open: Park, daily 11.00-17.00.
p 26
Rathlin Island reached from Ballycastle, Co Antrim.
p 18
Riber Castle Fauna Reserve, Matlock, Derbyshire.
Tel Matlock 2073.
Open: Daily 10.00-19.00 (until 16.00 in Winter).
pp 22, 46
Richmond Park, Richmond, Surrey.
p 25
Robertson Museum and Aquarium, Marine Station, Millport, Isle of Cumbrae, Strathclyde.
Tel Millport 581.
Open: Weekdays 9.30-12.30, 14.00-17.00. Closed Saturday in

Winter.
pp 2, 67
Robin Hill Country Park and Zoological Park, Robin Hill, Downend, Isle of Wight.
Tel Arreton 430.
Open: March-October 10.00-dusk.
p 38
Roe Valley Country Park, Limavady, Londonderry.
p 63
Rothesay Museum, 8 Bath Road, Bournemouth, Dorset. Tel Bournemouth 21009.
Open: Weekdays 10.30-17.00.
p 22
Royal Scottish Museum, Chambers Street, Edinburgh.
Tel 031 225 7534.
Open: Weekdays 10.00-17.00, Sunday 14.00-17.00.
p 66
Royal Windsor Safari Park, Windsor, Berkshire. Tel Windsor 69841.
Open: Daily 10.00-dusk.
pp 3, 34
Russell-Cotes Art Gallery and Museum, Russell-Cotes Road, Bournemouth BH1 3AA.
Tel Bournemouth 21009.
Open: Weekdays 10.30-17.00.
pp 2, 65

St Catherine's Island Zoo, Tenby, Dyfed.
Open: Easter-September daily 10.00-dusk (also depends on the tide).
p 42
St Ives Aquarium, Sloop Craft Market, St Ives, Cornwall.
p 3
Sandringham House, Estate Office, Sandringham, Norfolk. Tel Kings Lynn 2675.
Open: April-September, Tuesday-Thursday; May-August Sunday-Thursday 11.00-16.45 (from 12.00 on Sunday). Get in touch for details of closing.
p 26
Sandy Bay Leisure Complex, Exmouth, Devon.
Open: Daily 10.00-dusk.
p 39
Sandy Lodge Reserve, Sandy, Bedfordshire. Tel Sandy 80551.
Open: Monday-Friday 9.00-17.00, also Easter-end September Saturday 9.30-17.00. Sunday (members only).
pp 11, 18
Santon Downham Forest Walk, Brandon, Suffolk.
p 64
Saruman Museum, Beckley, nr Rye, Sussex. Tel Beckley 279.
Open: Daily 9.30-17.30.
p 21
Scarborough Zoo and Marineland, Northstead Manor Gardens, Scarborough, N Yorkshire.
Tel Scarborough 64401.
Open: Easter-October daily 10.00-dusk.
pp 3, 42
Scottish Fisheries Museum, St Ayles, Harbourhead, Anstruther.
Tel Anstruther 310628.
Open: April-October, weekdays 10.00-12.30, 14.00-18.00, Sunday 14.00-17.00, November-March daily (not Tuesday) 14.30-16.30.
pp 2, 65
Seal Sanctuary, Gweek, Cornwall.
Tel Mawgan 361.
Open: Daily 9.30-sunset.
p 31
Shane's Castle and Nature Reserve, Randalstown Road, Antrim.
Tel Antrim 3380.
Open: April-May, Sundays, Bank Holidays; June-August, Wednesday,

Saturday, Sunday, Bank Holidays; September, Sunday 13.00-19.00, Bank Holidays 13.00-19.00.
p 11

Skegness Natureland Marine Zoo, North Parade, The Promenade, Skegness, Lincolnshire.
Tel Skegness 4345.
Open: Daily June-October 10.00-19.30; October-May 10.00-16.00.
pp 3, 31, 42

Skeyton Farm Park, Primrose Farm, Skeyton, Norfolk.
Open: May, Sunday 11.00-18.00; June-September daily 11.00-18.00.
p 46

Skomer Island, c/o West Wales Naturalists' Trust, 4 Victoria Place, Haverfordwest, Dyfed.
Open: Easter-September, Tuesday-Sunday 10.00-16.00.
p 18

Slimbridge Branch of the Wildfowl Trust, Slimbridge, Gloucestershire.
Tel Cambridge (Glos) 333.
Open: Daily 9.30-17.30 or dusk.
p 19

Southam Wildlife Park, Southam, Warwickshire.
Tel Southam 2431.
Open: Easter-October daily 11.00-dusk.
p 42

Southampton Zoo, The Common, Southampton, Hampshire.
Tel Southampton 556603.
Open: Daily 10.00-18.00.
p 42

South Park, Darlington, Co Durham.
p 6

Southport Zoo, Princes Park, Southport, Lancashire.
Tel Southport 38102.
Open: Daily 10.00-dusk.
p 42

Spring Hill Wildfowl Park, Forest Row, E Sussex.
Tel Forest Row 2783.
Open: Daily 11.00-18.00.
p 6

Stagsden Bird Gardens, Stagsden, Bedfordshire.
Tel Oakley 2745.
Open: Daily 11.00-19.00 or dusk.
p 8

Stapleford Park, nr Melton Mowbray, Leicestershire.
Tel Wymondam 245.
Open: May-September, Sunday, Wednesday, Thursday, Summer Bank Holidays.
p 7

Stewartby Lake, Bedfordshire.
p 19

Stodmarsh National Nature Reserve, Stodmarsh, Kent.
p 19

Strangford Lough, Co Down.
p 19

Suffolk Wildlife Park, Kessingland, Suffolk.
Tel Lowestoft 740291.
Open: March-October daily 10.00-18.00 (or one hour before dusk).
p 40

Sundown Pets' Garden, Rampton, Retford, Nottinghamshire.
Tel Rampton 274.
Open: Daily (not Christmas Day or Boxing Day) 10.00-dusk.
p 42

Syon Park, Isleworth, Middlesex. Tel 01 560 0882.
Open: Daily, April-September 10.00-18.00; October-March 10.00-17.00 or dusk if sooner.
p 7

Tatton Park, Knutsford, Cheshire.

Tel Knutsford 3155.
Open: Tuesday-Sunday,
Bank Holiday Mondays (not
Christmas Day).
p 25

Teignmouth Aqualand,
Teignmouth, Devon.
Open: Easter-October daily.
p 3

Tentsmuir Point National Nature Reserve, Fife.
p 19

Thrapston Bird Gardens and Fish Centre, Thrapston,
Northamptonshire.
Open: Daily 10.30-dusk.
pp 3, 8

Threave House and Wildfowl Reserve, Castle Douglas,
Dumfries and Galloway.
Open: 9.00-sunset.
p 13

Tighnabruaich Wildlife Centre,
Tighnabruaich, Strathclyde.
p 46

Torbay Aqualand, Beacon Quay,
Torbay Harbour, Torbay, Devon.
Open: April-December.
p 3

Tower Buildings and Circus,
Blackpool, Lancashire.
Tel Blackpool 25252.
Open: May-October daily
9.30-23.00.
pp 2, 5, 23

Towner Art Gallery,
Manor House, 9 Borough Lane,
Eastbourne, Sussex.
Tel Eastbourne 21635.
Open: Weekdays 10.00-13.00,
14.00-17.00, Sunday 14.00-17.00.
pp 22, 66

Tring Zoological Museum,
Tring, Hertfordshire.
Tel Tring 4181.
Open: Weekdays 10.00-17.00,
Sunday 14.00-17.00.
pp 19, 67

Tropical Bird and Butterfly Gardens, Fentonluna Lane,
Padstow, Cornwall.
Tel Padstow 262.
Open: Daily 10.30-20.00.
pp 7, 23

Tropical Bird Gardens,
Rode, Frome, Somerset.
Tel Beckington 326.
Open: Daily, Summer
10.30-19.00; Winter 10.30 to
sunset.
p 8

Tropical Bird Park, Old Park,
St Lawrence, Isle of Wight.
Open: Daily 10.00-18.00.
p 8

Trust Visitor Centre, Torridon,
Highland.
pp 27, 64

Twycross Zoo, Twycross,
nr Atherstone,
Warwickshire.
Tel Tamworth 880250.
Open: Daily (not Christmas Day)
10.00-18.00 (until 16.00 in
Winter).
p 45

University Marine Biological Station,
Keppel Pier, Great Cumbrea Island,
Strathclyde.
Open: Easter-May, Monday-Friday
9.30-12.30, 14.00-17.00, Saturday
9.30-12.00; June-September,
weekdays 9.30-12.30, 14.00-17.00;
October-Easter, Monday-Friday
9.30-12.30, 14.00-17.00.
p 2

University Museum of Zoology,
Downing Street, Cambridge.
Open: Monday-Friday 14.15-17.15.
p 65

Vale of Dedham Heavy Horse Centre, Dedham, Colchester,
Essex. Tel Colchester 322142.
Open: Easter-October Sunday
11.00-16.00.
p 44

Vane Farm, Loch Leven, nr Kinross, Tayside.
Open: November-March, Saturday and Sunday 11.00-16.30; April-October Saturday-Thursday 11.00-17.00.
pp 10, 63

Vane Farm Nature Reserve, Loch Leven, nr Kinross. Tayside.
Open: April-September Saturday-Thursday 9.30-17.00; October-March Saturday-Tuesday 9.30-16.30.
pp 16, 63

Verne Estate Garden and Aviaries, Marden, Hereford and Worcester.
Tel Bodenham 232.
Open: Daily.
p 7

Waddesdon Manor, Waddesdon, Buckinghamshire.
Tel Waddesdon 211.
Open: Good Friday-October, Wednesday-Sunday 14.00-18.00, Bank Holidays 11.00-18.00 (grounds and aviary Sunday from 11.00).
pp 8, 27

Washington Branch of the Wildfowl Trust, Middle Barmston Farm, Washington, Tyne and Wear.
Tel Washington 465454.
Open: Daily 9.30-dusk (until 21.00 in June-August). Closed Christmas Eve and Christmas Day.
p 19

Wellplace Bird Farm, Ipsden, Oxfordshire. Tel Checkendon 680473.
Open: End March-September, Monday-Friday from 13.30, Saturday, Sunday from 10.00; October-March, Saturday and Sunday from 10.00.
pp 7, 45

Welney Branch of the Wildfowl Trust, Welney, Norfolk.
Open: Daily 13.00-17.00 (escorted visits Saturday, Sunday 10.00, 13.45).
p 19

Welsh Mountain Zoo, Colwyn Bay, Clwyd.
Tel Colwyn Bay 2938.
Open: April-October daily 9.30-19.00; October-March 10.00-16.00.
pp 28, 38

West Country Wildlife Park, Cricket St Thomas, Somerset.
Open: Daily 10.00-18.00 or dusk.
p 38

West Midland Safari Park, Spring Grove, Bewdley, Hereford and Worcester. Tel Bewdley 402114.
Open: Mid March-October daily 10.00-17.00.
pp 2, 33

West Wales Farm Park, Blawnbedwlsaf, nr Llandyssul, Dyfed. Tel Rhydlewis 317.
p 45

Weyhill European Wildlife Park, Weyhill, nr Andover, Hampshire.
Tel Weyhill 2252.
Open: Daily 10.30-18.00 (until 16.00 in winter).
p 46

Whipsnade Zoo, Whipsnade, Bedfordshire. Tel Whipsnade 872171.
Open: Daily 10.00-18.00 or sunset.
pp 3, 43

Whitcliffe Wood, nr Ludlow, Shropshire.
p 26

Whitson Zoological Park, Whitson Court, Newport, Gwent.
Tel Newport 72515.
Open: April-September daily 10.00-18.00.
p 41

Wicken Fen, nr Soham, Cambridgeshire.
Open: Throughout the year. You

are asked to sign the visitors' book at the National Trust shop at the Keeper's House.
Shop open: 10.00-13.00, 14.00-18.00 (until 16.00 in winter). Closed Thursday.
p 20

Widcombe Bird Gardens, Blagdon Hill, Somerset.
Tel Blagdon Hill 268.
Open: April-October daily 10.30-17.30 (gardens close 19.00).
p 5

Wild Life Country Park, Lowther, Penrith, Cumbria. Tel Hackthorpe 392.
Open: April-June, September 10.00-17.00; July and August 10.00-18.00.
p 45

Wirral Country Park Visitor Centre, Thurstanton, Wirral, Cheshire. Tel 051 648 4371.
Open: April, May, September, October 10.30-17.00; June-August 10.30-20.00; November-March 10-30-15.30.
p 64

Witley Common Information Centre, Witley, Surrey.
Open: Easter-October, Bank Holiday Mondays, Tuesday-Thursday 11.00-17.00, Saturday, Sunday 11.00-16.00.
p 64

Woburn Wild Animal Kingdom, Woburn Park, Bedfordshire.
Tel Woburn 246.
Open: Winter daily 12.00-16.00; Summer Monday-Saturday 10.30-17.45, Sunday 10.00-18.15; Autumn Monday-Saturday 11.00-17.15, Sunday 11.00-17.45.
pp 3, 34

Wollaton Hall *see* Nottingham Natural History Museum.

Worldwide Butterflies Ltd, Compton House, Over Compton, Sherbourne, Dorset.
Tel Yeovil 4608.
Open: Easter-October daily 10.00-17.00.
p 22

Wyre Forest Visitor Information Centre, Bewdley, Shropshire.
Open: Easter-end September, Tuesday, Thursday, Saturday, Sunday 13.00-17.00; October-Easter, Saturday and Sunday 13.00-dusk.
p 62

Yafford Mill, nr Shorwell, Isle of Wight.
Tel Brightstone 740610.
Open: Easter-September weekdays 10.00-18.00, Sunday 12.00-18.00.
p 31

Yorkshire Dales National Park Information Centre, Clapham, N Yorkshire. Tel Clapham 419.
Open: April-September daily mid morning-late afternoon.
p 63

Zetland Museum, King Street, Redcar, Cleveland.
Tel Redcar 71921.
Open: Weekdays 10.00-17.30.
pp 3, 67